SIDDUR BAYIT

THE BELIEVERS HEBREW
PRAYER COMPANION

NMZ
BOOKS

Copyright © 2014 by NO MANS ZONE
Publishing history: Edition 2014
Cover Design by NO MANS ZONE

All Scripture quotations in this publication are from the RSTNE *(Restoration Scriptures True Name Edition.* Your Arms to Yisrael Publishing 2004 unless otherwise indicated.

Publisher's Disclaimer

All rights reserved. No portion of this publication may be reproduced, stored in an electronic system, or transmitted in any form or by any means, electronic, mechanical, photocopy, recording, or otherwise, without permission in writing from the publisher. Brief quotations may be used in literary reviews. Whilst every care has been taken to ensure the accuracy of the material contained herein, neither the author nor the publisher or its agents will accept responsibility or liability for any action taken by any person, persons or organisation claimed to be in whole or in part upon the information contained herein.

Proceeds from the publication, distribution and sale of this book are received as gifts to NO MANS ZONE.

ISBN-13:978-1478136583

Published by

NO MANS ZONE
PO 107099
Auckland Airport
New Zealand 2150
www.nomanszone.org

A publication of

NO MANS ZONE

DEDICATION

This Siddur Bayit is dedicated to the Kohanim (Priests)

ACKNOWLEDEMENT

NMZ would like to acknowledge and thank the authors of all publications, translations and other works cited in this Siddur.

PREFACE

The Siddur Bayit has been complied for individuals or families who have no access to a Synagogue or a Fellowship where Hebrew or Hebraic teaching is available. It has been designed for the non-Hebrew reader. The sons and daughters of YHWH (the Elohim of Yisra'el) who are in exile awaiting Aliyah (a return to Yisra'el). As believers in YHWH it is our duty to learn the customs of our forefathers in the Hebrew Faith.

The intention of the Siddur Bayit is to encourage you to practice and participate in keeping the Morning, Noon and Evening Prayers, the Blessings, Dedications, Proclamations and Intercessions of which are essential to developing and maintaining your identity as an Irvit (a Hebrew believer) in the Elohim (Creator) of Avraham (Abraham), Yitzchak (Isaac), Yaakov (Jacob).

The word "Siddur" means order and the word "Bayit" means house therefore, literally a Siddur for the home.

The Hebrew of the Bayit Siddur is transliterations of the original Hebrew texts and is best sounded out using the transliteration keys at the start of this Siddur. Please do not by pass the Hebrew but rather give it your best and you will become familiar with the Hebrew very quickly and it will help you later to learn how to pronounce the Hebrew texts proficiently.

NOTICE

A special note on the pronunciation of the Set Apart Name of the Father

In Hebrew the Set Apart Name is composed of four letters YHWH pronounced as Yud י, Hei ה, Vav ו, Hei ה.

This is referred to as the "Tetragram" or "Tetragrammaton" meaning roughly, "The Four Letters" - YHWH.

How the Tetragram is actually pronounced their is no general consensus among scholars.

Current research points to one of five related pronunciations for the Set Apart Name:

1) *Yah-way*
2) *Yah-hoo-way*
3) *Yah-oo-ay*
4) *Yah-oo-ah*
5) *Yeh-ho-vah*

For this the English version of the Tetragram YHWH and the Hebrew "YHWH" is employed throughout this Siddur to allow the reader to follow his or her own convictions on the pronunciation of the Sacred Name.

The term LORD or Lord as it is used in English Bible translations is a substitute of the Tetragam therefore it is not employed in this Siddur.

Other terms that is used in this Siddur

Yeshua (alternatively Yahushua): this is the eternal name of the Son whom in Christianity is called Jesus.

Ruach haKodesh: this is the eternal name of the set apart Spirit of the Father whom in Christianity is called the Holy Spirit.

Elohim: This is translated in our English Bibles as God. We prefer the term Creator.

Eloha: The singular of Elohim.

Adonai: This is translated as Sovereign or Master.

Kahal: the Hebrew name for congregation/assembly or what Christianity calls the Church.

Mitzrayim: The Hebrew name for Egypt or more correctly an ancient place that was located in Saudi Arabia of which is symbolic of ancient Egypt.

Yahrushalayim: More accurately called Yerushalem from whence we get the name Jerusalem.

Amein: Literally, so be it.

This Siddur has been written as a guide and you are free to skip, insert and change any part you may find appropriate or inappropriate for your situation. However, we do recommend that you first learn the pattern and then adjust accordingly.

Note: The parts in the "grey colour" are informational and it is there as a guide, these should not be read out during the Prayer.

We have employed the RSTNE translation in this Siddur;

RSTNE *(Restoration Scriptures True Name Edition)*, 2004. Your Arms to Yisrael Publishing.

TRANSLITERATION KEY

ch - as in ba**ch**

kh - as in ba**rk**

ki - as in **key**

tz - as in pit**zz**a

oo - as in b**oo**t

ay - as in b**ay**

y - as in m**y**

a - as in m**a**

e - as in **eh**

i - as in h**i**

el - as in **ayl**

ee - as in b**ee**t

oe - as in t**oe**

When letters appear on their own for example "b" in *b'Mitz'votav* it is pronounced as how the letter is sounded in English "bur".

When a semi-colon " ' " appears in a word for example *ham'vorakh* it indicates a break in the sounding of the word.

CONTENTS

MIKVEH...1
The Blessing before immersing in Water

SHEMEN HA-MISCHAH...............................3
The Blessing of the Anointing Oil

TALLIT...5
The Blessing before putting on a Tallit

TEFFILIN..6
The Blessing before putting on Teffilin

SHOFAR...8
The Blessing before blowing a Shofar

SHEMA..9
The Declaration of Faith

ASERET HA-DEVARIM................................11
The Ten Words

TIFILLAT TALMID.......................................14
The Disciple Prayer

TORAH EMET..17
The Essenic Torah

HA-SHACRIT...20
The Morning Prayers

HA-MINCHAH..25
The Morning Prayers

HA-MA'ARIV..28
The Evening Prayers

MA TOV...33
O How Good

HALELU B'SHAYM..34
The Praising of the Great Name

MIKRA YERUSHALEM..................................43
Proclamation for Yerushalem

MIKRA YISRAEL..48
Proclamation for Yisra'el

AZ YASHIR MOSHE.......................................55
The Song of Moshe

AMIDAH..60
The Weekly Prayer

SHABBAT AMIDAH..71
The Shabbat Prayer

EIN KELOHEINU..76
There is none like our Elohim

ASREI...77
The Weekly Psalm

AVINU MALKEINU..79
Our Father, our King

KADDISH...82
The Mourner's Prayer

BIRKHOT AHARONIC...................................85
The Aharonic Priestly Blessing

HA-TORAH..86
The Blessing before and after reading Torah

HAFTORAH...87

The Blessing before and after reading the
Prophets

HA-TEHILLIM...89
The Blessing before and after reading the Psalms

KETUVIM NETZARIM....................................90
The Blessing before and after reading the
Renewed Covenant

BIRAT HAMAZON...91
The Blessing after Meals

BIRKHOT...93
The General Blessings

MEZUZAH...101
The Blessing for the Mezuzah

ABOUNT NOMANSZONE...............................102

MIKVEH

The term mikveh in Hebrew literally means any gathering of waters, but is specifically used in Jewish law for the waters or bath for the ritual immersion. Immersion in water is symbolic of both a spiritual death and a rebirth. As one is immersed in water, this is representative of dying to the old nature that leads one to sin; as one emerges from the water this is representative of a new beginning. At mikveh one reaffirms their acceptance of the Torah by declaring, *"I will hear and I will do"* which was a phrase from the oath that was originally taken by the priests not to forsake the Torah (Devarim (Deuteronomy) 29:9-14). It was a practice among the early believers to mikveh at least once a day. One should immerse every day except on the Shabbat and it can be done in the sea or in a shower or tub if there is no mikvah.

MIKVAH

Full Immersion

Before immersing three times say:

Barukh Atah יהוה, *Eloheinu Melech haOlam, Asher kidshanu b'mitzvotav v'tzivanu al mitzvat mikvah.*

Praised are You YHWH, our Elohim King of the Universe, Who sanctified us with Mitzvot, and commands us concerning the commandment of immersion.

After immersing three times say:

Shema Yisra'el.

I will hear and I will do.

Siddur Bayit

In Hebrew understanding it is more important to obey the commandments than know why. As we obey the commandments its purpose and understanding will follow as we are faithful.

The Believers Hebrew Prayer Companion

SHEMEN HA-MISCHAH

The set apart anointing oil (Hebrew: *shemen* "oil", *ha'mishchah* "of anointing" formed an integral part of the ordination of the the High Priest (*Kohen haGogodal*) and (*kohanim*) priests and the consecration of the articles of the mishkan (tabernacle) (Shemoth (Exodus) 30:26) and subsequent Temples in Yerushalem. The primary purpose of anointing with the set apart anointing oil was to cause the anointed persons or objects to become *qodesh* – most set apart (Shemoth (Exodus) 30:29).

Originally the oil was used exclusively for the kohanim (priests) and the Tabernacle furnitures but was later extended to include navim (prophets) and melekim (kings). It was forbidden to be used on a stranger (Shemoth (Exodus) 30:33) or to be used on the body of any common persons and the Israelites were forbidden to duplicate any like it for themselves (Shemoth (Exodus) 30:32). This prohibition applied while the Temple was in service.

Shemoth (Exodus) 30:22-37 lists the ingredients of the anointing oil as follows:

1. Liquid myrrh,
2. Sweet-smelling cinnamon (a kind of cinnamon of the laurel family),
3. Aromatic cane (sweet cane or sugar cane),
4. Cassia (inner bark of cinnamon),
5. Olive oil.

The anointing oil is available for purchased from Israel via the internet. If you are not able to obtain it from Israel then inquire locally among believers otherwise you may create a batch according to the above description.

BIRKAT SHEMEN HA-MISHCHAH

The prayer of sanctification of the anointing oil

Barukh Atah יהוה, *Eloheinu Melech haOlam, Asher kidshanu b'mitzvotav v'tzivanu al mitzvat shemen ha'mishchah.*

Praised are You YHWH, our Elohim King of the Universe, Who sanctified us with Mitzvot, and commands us concerning the commandment of the anointing oil.

TALLIT

A Tallit is a scarflike rectangular prayer shawl. From each of its four corners a tasselled fringe is attached and suspended, these tassels are called in Hebrew *tzitzit*. See Bamidbar (Numbers) 15:39. A Tallit is traditionally worn at morning or evening prayers. You can purchase one from the internet or alternatively can make one using a plain white clothe which should not be a mixture of linen and wool or other fabrics. See Wayiqra (Leviticus) 19:19. At each corner of the shawl attach a tassel according to the pattern in Bamidbar (Numbers) 15:38.

TALLIT

The prayer shawl

Before putting on the Tallit anoint yourself with anointing oil then anoint the four tassels on the four corners of your Tallit. Unfold the Tallit and face the *Atarah* (the collar of the tallit where the blessing is written) towards you. Kiss the corner of the Atarah.

Then recite the blessing:

Barukh Atah יהוה, *Eloheinu Melech haOlam, Asher kidshanu b'mitzvotav v'tzivanu lit'atayf batzitzit.*

Praised are You YHWH, our Elohim King of the Universe, Who sanctified us with Mitzvot, and commands us to wrap ourselves in tzitzit.

TEFILLIN

The word *Tefillin* is commonly translated as "phylacteries." Tefillin are two small black boxes with black straps attached to them; the box that is attached to the arm is called *Shel Yad* and the box that is attached to the forehead is called *Shel Rosh*. The text that is inserted inside the two boxes of Tefillin is hand-written by a scribe, and consists of the four sets of biblical verses in which Tefillin are commanded (Shemoth (Exodus) 13:1-10, 11-16; Devarim (Deuteronomy) 6:4-9, 11:13-21). Tefillin are meant to remind us of YHWH's mitzvot. Certain Jewish groups the Karaites and ancient Sadducees understood these verses to be figurative; it means only that one should always be preoccupied with words of Torah, as if they were in front of one's eyes, for this reason many do not practice Tefillin but that should not stop one from saying the prayers only for purpose of acknowledging the commandment. Tefillin are wrapped around the arm seven times, and the straps on the head are adjusted so they fit snugly. Ashkenazi Jews and Sefardi Jews have different traditions on how they put on Tefillin. Sefardi stand while putting on Shel Yad and Shel Rosh, Ashkenazi sit. Sefardi wrap away from the body and Ashkenazi warp towards the body.

TEFILLIN MITZVOT

The phylacteries commandment

Before tightening the strap around the arm say:

Barukh Atah יהוה, Eloheinu Melech haOlam, Asher kidshanu b'mitzvotav v'tzivanu l'hani'ach tefillin.

Praised are You YHWH, our Elohim King of the Universe, Who sanctified us with Mitzvot, and commands us to put on tefillin.

Before tightening the strap around the head say:

Barukh shem k'vod malkhuto l'olam va'ed.

Praised is the name of His glorious Kingdom forever and ever.

This prayer is said as a meditation as you wrap the strap around the middle finger three times.

V'ayra'teekh lee l'olam,

V'ayra'teekh lee b'tzadek

uv'mispat uv'chesaid uv'rachameem,

V'ayras'teekh lee be'emuna v'yada'at et יהוה.

I will wed You to me forever. I will wed You to me with right and justice, with love and mercy. I will wed You to me with faith and you shall Know YHWH.

SHOFAR

The shofar is an instrument most often made from a ram's horn, though it can also be made from the horn of a sheep or goat. It makes a trumpet-like sound and is traditionally blown on Yom Teruah, Yom Kippur and the Jewish holiday of Rosh haShanah (the Jewish New Year). It may also be blown on the Shabbat as part of the Shabbat evening prayers following the *Amidah* (see section on Shabbat Amidah).

BIRKAT SHOFAR

The prayer of sanctification of the shofar

Barukh Atah יהוה, Eloheinu Melech haOlam, Asher kidshanu b'mitzvotav v'tzivanu al mitzvat shofar.

Praised are You YHWH, our Elohim King of the Universe, Who sanctified us with Mitzvot, and commands us concerning the commandment of the shofar.

SHEMA

The Shema is the most important declaration of faith in YHWH in the Scriptures. Most people pray the Shema as part of their weekly morning or evening prayer. We say the Shema standing facing Yerushalem. Some put their hand over their right eye in the form of the Hebrew letter Shin.

THE SHEMA

The declaration of Yisra'el

Face Yerushalem and say:

Shema Yisra'el יהוה Eloheinu, יהוה Echad!
(Softly) Barukh sheim k'vod mal'khuto l'olam va'ed!

Hear, O Yisra'el: YHWH is our Elohim, the Eternal YHWH alone! (Devarim (Deuteronomy) 6:4) Praised is YHWH's glorious majesty forever and ever!

V'ahavta ayt יהוה Elohekhah, b'khol l'vav'kha uv'khol nafish'kha uv'khol m'dekha. V'ha'yu had'varim ha'aylay asher anokhee m'tzav'kha hayom al l'vavekha. V'shinantam l'vanekha v'dibarta bam, b'shivt'kha b'vaytekha uvlekht'kha baderekh uv, shokhb'kha uv'kumekha. Uk'shartam l'ot al yadekha v'hayu l'totafot bayn aynekha. Ukh'tavtam al m'zuzot baytekha uvish'arekha. L'ma'an tizk'ru va'asitem et kol mitzvotai Vihyeetem k'doshim layloheikhem.
Ani יהוה Eloheikhem asher hotzaytee et'khem may'eretz
Mitzrayim Lihyot lakhem laylohem.
Ani יהוה Eloheikhem.

And you shall love YHWH your Elohim with all your lev, and with all your being, and with all your might.
And these words, which I command you this day, shall be in your lev: And you shall teach them diligently to your children, and

shall talk of them when you sit in your bayit, and when you walk by the way, and when you lie down, and when you rise up. And you shall bind them for an ot upon your hand, and they shall be as frontlets between your eyes. And you shall write them upon the posts of your bayit, and on your gates. That you may remember, and do all My mitzvoth, and be kadosh to your Elohim.
I am YHWH your Elohim, Who brought you out of the land of Mitzrayim, to be your Elohim: I am YHWH your Elohim.

Devarim (Deuteronomy) 6:5-9, Bamidbar (Numbers) 15:40-41.

AHAVTA RE'ECHA KHAMOKHA

V'ah havta l'ray kha khamokha. Ani יהוה.

And you shall love your neighbor as yourself: I am YHWH.

Wayiqra (Leviticus) 19:18.

ASERET HA-DEVARIM

THE DECALOGUE

The Ten Words

In Rabbinical Hebrew it is known as *Aseret haDibrot* or the ten words. The Decalogue (Devarim (Deuteronomy) 5:6-21) was originally part of the daily prayers of the early believers because it was written on some old Tefillin and the doors posts of some houses. It is a mitzvah (commandment) to recite the Decalogue daily. See Devarim (Deuteronomy) 6. One in which YHWH attaches many great promises and abundant blessings.

Anokhee יהוה Elohekha asher hotzayteekha may'eretz mitzrayim mibayit avadim.

I am YHWH your Elohim, Who brought you out of the land of Mitzrayim, from the bayit of slavery.

Lo yihyay-l'kha elohim achayrim al-panai lo ta'asay-l'kha fesel v'khol-t'munah asher bashamayim mima'al va'asher ba'aretz mitachat va'saher bamayim mitachat la'aretz lo tistachavay lahem v'lo to'ov'daym ki anokhee יהוה Elohekha El kana pokayd avon avot al-baneen al-shilayshim v'al-ribay'im l'son'aivosay chesaid la'alaphim l'ohavai ul'shom'ray mitzvotai.

You shall have no other elohim before My face.
You shall not make any graven image, or any likeness of anything that is in the shamayim above, or that is on the earth beneath, or that is in the mayim beneath the earth:
You shall not bow down to them, nor serve them: for I YHWH your Elohim am a jealous El, visiting the iniquity of the ahvot upon the children to the third and fourth generation of those Who hate Me, And showing rachamim to thousands of those Who love Me and shomer My mitzvoth.

Lo tisa et-shaym- יהוה Elohehka lashav ki lo y'nakay יהוה ayt asher-yisa et-sh'mo lashav.

You shall not bring the Name of YHWH your Elohim to vain emptiness: for YHWH will not hold him guiltless that brings His Name to vain emptiness.

Zakhor et-yom hashabat l'kad'sho shayshet yamim ta'avod v'aseeta khol-m'laktekha v'yom hash'vi'I Shabbat l' יהוה Elohekah lo ta'say khol-m'lakhah Atah uvin'kha-uvitekha avd'kha va'amat'kha v'gayr'kha asher bish'arekah ki shayshet yameen asah יהוה et-hashamayim v'et-ha'aretz et-hayam v'et-kol-asher-bam vayanach bayom hash'vi'i al-kayn bayrakh יהוה et-yom hashabat va-y'kad'shayhu.

Shomer Yom ha Shabbat to set it apart, as YHWH your Elohim has commanded you.
Six days you shall labour, and do all your work: But the seventh day is the Shabbat of YHWH your Elohim: in it you shall not do any work, you, nor your son, nor your daughter, nor your male eved, nor your female eved, nor your ox, nor your donkey, nor any of your cattle, nor the ger that is within your gates; that your male eved and your female eved may rest as well as you. And remember that you were an eved in the land of Mitzrayim, and that YHWH your Elohim brought you out from there through a mighty hand and by an outstretched Arm: therefore YHWH your Elohim commanded you to shomer Yom ha Shabbat.

Kabayd et-aveekha v'et-imekah l'ma'an ya'areekhun yamekha al ha'adamah asher- יהוה Elohekha notayn lakh.

Honour your abba and your eema, as YHWH your Elohim has commanded you; that your days may be prolonged, and that it may go well with you, in the land that YHWH your Elohim gives you.

Lo tirtzach. Lo tin'af. Lo tignov. Lo ta'anay b'ray'akha ayd shaker.

You shall not murder. Neither shall you commit adultery. Neither shall you steal. Neither shall you bear false witness against your neighbour.

Lo tachmod bayit ray'ekha lo-tachmod ayshet ray'ekha
V'avdo va'amato v'shoro vachamoro v'khol asher l'ray'ekha.
Amein.

Neither shall you desire your neighbour's wife, neither shall you covet your neighbour's bayit, his field, nor his male eved, nor his female eved, his ox, or his donkey, or anything that is your neighbour's. Amein.

TIFILLAT TALMID

The Tifillat Tamid literally means "Disciple's Prayer" (Mattityahu (Mathew) 6:9-15. It is believed that this prayer is an abbreviation of the *Amidah* (See Amidah section). The disciple's prayer can be said as part of the morning prayer or evening prayer. This is how Yeshua would have taught it to the disciple's because He would have said it in *Leshon haKodesh* or Torah Hebrew the language of prayer.

TIFILLAT TALMID

The disciple's prayer

Aveinu Shebashamayim yitkadash Sh'mekah.

Our Abba Who is in the shamayim, kadosh shmecha.

Tavo mal'khutekha yay'asay ratzon'kha k'mo bashamayim kayn ba'aretz.

Your malchut come. Your ratzon be done in the earth, as it is in the shamayim.

Et-lechem chukaynu ten-lanu hayom.

Give us today our daily lechem.

Us'lach-lanu et-chovotaynu ka'asher salachnu gam-anachnu lacha-yavanu.

And forgive us our debts, as we forgive our debtors.

Va'al tavee'aynu leeday nisayon ki im-chal'tzaynu min-hara ki l'kah hamamlakha v'hagavura v'hatif'eret l'ol'may olameen. Amein.

And lead us not into temptation, but deliver us from evil: For Yours is the malchut, and the power, and the tifereth, le-olam-va-ed. Amein.

THE TEN REVERSALS

The Beatitudes

The Beatitudes of Mattityahu (Mathew) 5:2-12 is more than just a blessing. In Hebrew it is called the ten reversals of Hoshea (Hosea) chapter 1 where YHWH pronounced a threefold curse on Yisra'el which was as follows (1) *Yizre-El* means El scatter - El will sow (2) *Lo'Ruhamah* means no compassion - no mercy (3) *Lo'Ami* means not my people. In the Beatitudes Yeshua crushed and reversed this curse on Yisra'el with this tenfold blessing.

Ashray aneeay ruach lahem malakhut hashamayim.

Blessed are the poor in ruach: for theirs is the malchut ha shamayim.

Ashray ha'avaylim ki haym yanuchamu.

Blessed are they that mourn: for they shall be comforted.

Asray ha'anavim ki hayma yiyrshu ha'aretz.

Blessed are the meek: for they shall inherit the Land.

Ashray har'ayvim vahatzmay'im la'tzedakah ki haym yisba'u.

Blessed are they that do hunger and thirst after tzedakah: for they shall be filled.

Ashray ha'rachamanim ki haym yaruchamu.

Blessed are the rachamim givers: for they shall obtain rachamim.

Ashray baray layvav ki haym yechezu et ha'Elohim.

Blessed are the pure in lev: for they shall see Elohim.

Asray rodafee shalom ki banay Elohim yiqaray'u.

Blessed are the shalom-makers: for they shall be called b'nai Elohim.

Ashray hanir'dafim al davar ha'tzedaka ki lahem malkhut hashamayim.

Blessed are those who are persecuted for tzedakah's sake: for theirs is the malchut ha shamayim.

Asharakhem im yicharafu etakhem veedabru vasheker Aleikem kol ra ba'avuree.

Blessed are you, when men shall revile you, and persecute you, and shall say all manner of evil against you falsely, for My sake.

Simachu vageelu ki sakhrakhem rav bashamayim ki khayn radafu et ha'navim asher hainu lifnaykhem. Amein.

Gilah, and be in great simcha: for great is your reward in the shamayim: for so persecuted they the Nevim who were before you. Amein.

MOSHIACH BIRKAT

The blessing of the Messiah

Barukh Atah יהוה, Eloheinu Melech haOlam, Asher natan lanu et dereck ha-Yeshua b' Moshiach.

Praised are You YHWH, our Elohim King of the Universe, Who has given us the way of salvation in Messiah Yeshua.

Barukh haba b'shaym יהוה, Hal'luyah!

Praised is He Who comes in the name of YHWH, Halleluyah!

TORAH EMET

In 1881 an English minister by the name of Rev. G. J. Ouseley, obtained a copy of the Besorah (gospel) that appears to be the original version from which the present copies of "the New Testament" are derived. It was preserved in a Tibetan Monastery by the Essenes where it was hidden for two millennia for safety from the hands of the corrupters. It was translated from the Aramaic by Rev Ouseley and given the name "The Gospel of the Holy Twelve."

It is our conclusion after a careful comparison of the passages of this Besorah with the Roman version that the image of Yeshua that is presented in this Besorah and the message He teaches in this Besorah bears all the signs of an original Besorah but it has its contentions. The entire message of this Besorah is summarized in this teaching which we have compiled into a Hebraic prayer which we have called "the Torah Emet" (the Original Torah). It is also a declaration of faith.

TORAH EMET

The Essenic Torah

Barukh Atah יהוה, *Eloheinu Melech haOlam, Asher diber-lanu k'Yeshua Hamasheeach asher d'var hachayim.*

Praised are You YHWH, our Elohim King of the Universe, Who has spoken to us as Yeshua the Messiah, Who is the word of life.

And Yeshua said unto them, "Behold, anew I give unto you, the Torah Emet (The Torah of Truth), which is not new but from old. Even as Moshe gave the Torah to Yisra'el after the flesh, so also I give unto You the Torah Emet for the Malchut (Kingdom) of Yisra'el after the Ruach (Spirit).

For who are the Yisra'el of Elohim (Creator)? Even they of every

Siddur Bayit

nation and tribe who work tzedakah (righteousness), ahava (love), rachamim (mercy) and keep my Mitzvot (Commandments) these are the true Yisra'el of Elohim."

And standing upon his feet, Yeshua Spake, saying:

1. "Hear, O Yisra'el: YHWH is our Elohim, the Eternal YHWH alone! Many are My shlichim (apostles), and My navim (Prophets). In Me all live and move, and have subsistence.
2. Ye shall love YHWH with all your understanding of Torah kadosh (set apart Torah).
3. Ye shall love thy neighbour as yourself, even as the Torah kadosh instructs.
4. Ye shall not take away the life of any creature for your pleasure, nor for your profit, nor yet torment it.
5. Ye shall not steal the goods of any, nor gather lands and riches to yourselves, beyond your need or use.
6. Ye shall not eat the flesh, nor drink the blood of any slaughtered creature, nor yet anything which bringeth disorder to your health or senses.
7. Ye shall not make impure marriages, where love and health are not, nor yet corrupt yourselves, or any creature made pure by haKadosh (the Set Apart Spirit).
8. Ye shall not bear false witness against any, nor wilfully deceive any by a lie to hurt them.
9. Ye shall not do unto others, as ye would not that others should do unto you.
10. Ye shall worship En Sof Echad (the limitless and endless One), Avinu – Emma, (Father and Mother) in the Shamayim (Heaven), of Whom are all things, and reverence the Kadosh (Set Apart) Name YHWH, keeping sacred their daily kadosh tefillot (set apart prayers).
11. Ye shall revere your Avot (Fathers) and your Emot (Mothers) on earth, whose care is for you, and all the Teachers of Tzedakah (Righteousness).
12. Ye shall cherish and protect the weak, and those who are oppressed, and all creatures that suffer wrong.
13. Ye shall work with your hands the things that are tov (good) and seemly, so shalt ye eat the fruits of ha'aretz (the land) and live long in the Olam (Earth).

14. Ye shall mikvah (immerse) purify yourselves daily and rest every Yom Shabbat (the Sabbath day) from labour, keeping kadosh the Rosh Chodesh (New Moon celebrations), Chag (Festivals) and the Moedim (Feasts) of your Elohim and Boreh (Creator).
15. Ye shall do unto others, as ye would that others should unto you.

And when his disciples heard these kadosh words, they smote upon their breasts, saying: "Wherein we have offended, O YHWH please forgive us; and may thy chochmah, ahava and emet within us, so incline our hearts to love, keep and cherish this Torah Emet."

Barukh Atah יהוה, Eloheinu Melech haOlam, Asher asah et d'varo or lagoyim v'yaysha l'Yisra'el.

Praised are You YHWH, our Elohim King of the Universe, Who has made His word a light to the nations and salvation to Yisra'el.

HA-SHACRIT

These are prayers that we make when arising in the morning. These prayers thank YHWH for His faithfulness and His mercy that we are alive today that we are healthy and strong and able to do the most menial of tasks like getting dressed and putting on our shoes. Some of these prayers are of rabbinical origin and some are ancient. Ha'Shacrit means the Morning Prayer.

TALLIT

The prayer shawl

While holding the Tallit in your hand say:

Barukh Atah יהוה, *Eloheinu Melech haOlam, Asher kidshanu b'mitzvotav v'tzivanu lit'atayf batzitzit.*

Praised are You YHWH, our Elohim King of the Universe, Who sanctified us with Mitzvot, and commands us to wrap ourselves in tzitzit.

THE SHEMA

The declaration of Yisra'el

Face Yerushalem and say:

Shema Yisra'el יהוה *Eloheinu,* יהוה *Echad!*
(Softly) *Barukh sheim k'vod mal'khuto l'olam va'ed!*

Hear, O Yisra'el: YHWH is our Elohim, the Eternal YHWH alone! Devarim – Deuteronomy 6:4 Praised is YHWH's glorious majesty forever and ever!

V'ahavta ayt יהוה *Elohekhah, b'khol l'vav'kha uv'khol nafish'kha uv'khol m'dekha. V'hayu had'varim ha'aylay asher anokhee*

m'tzav'kha hayom al l'vavekha. V'shinantam l'vanekha v'dibarta bam, b'shivt'kha b'vaytekha uvlekht'kha baderekh uv, shokhb'kha uv'kumekha. Uk'shartam l'ot al yadekha v'hayu l'totafot bayn aynekha. Ukh'tavtam al m'zuzot baytekha uvish'arekha. L'ma'an tizk'ru va'asitem et kol mitzvotai Vihyeetem k'doshim laylohaykhem.
Ani יהוה Elohaykhem asher hotzaytee et'khem may'eretz Mitzrayim Lihyot lakhem laylohim.
Ani יהוה Elohaykhim. V'ah havta l'ray kha khamokha. Ani יהוה.

And you shall love YHWH your Elohim with all your lev, and with all your being, and with all your might. And these words, which I command you this day, shall be in your lev: And you shall teach them diligently to your children, and shall talk of them when you sit in your bayit, and when you walk by the way, and when you lie down, and when you rise up. And you shall bind them for an ot upon your hand, and they shall be as frontlets between your eyes. And you shall write them upon the posts of your bayit, and on your gates. That you may remember, and do all My mitzvoth, and be kadosh to your Elohim.
I am YHWH your Elohim, Who brought you out of the land of Mitzrayim, to be your Elohim: I am YHWH your Elohim.
And you shall love your neighbor as yourself: I am YHWH.

BIRKHOT HA-SHACRIT

The morning blessings

In Hebrew we always praise or bless the originator and creator of life YHWH and not the subject or object of His creation.

El Melech ne'eman.

El my trustworthy King.

Modeh Ani l'fanekha Melech chai v'kayam,
Shehechezarta bi nish'mati b'chem'lah. Rabah emunatecha.

I give thanks to You my King, for returning my soul to me in mercy. Great is Your faithfulness.

Barukh Atah יהוה, Eloheinu Melech haOlam, Asher natan lasekh'vi veenah l'hav'cheen bayn yom uvayn lailah.

Praised are You YHWH, our Elohim King of the Universe, Who has given the mind the ability to distinguish day from night.

Barukh Atah יהוה, Eloheinu Melech haOlam, She'asani b'tzelem Elohim.

Praised are You YHWH, our Elohim King of the Universe, Who has made me in the image of Elohim.

Barukh Atah יהוה, Eloheinu Melech haOlam, She'asani Yisra'el.

Praised are You YHWH, our Elohim King of the Universe, Who has made me an Israelite.

Barukh Atah יהוה, Eloheinu Melech haOlam, She'asani ben/bat chorin.

Praised are You YHWH, our Elohim King of the Universe, Who has made me (male/female) to be free.

Barukh Atah יהוה, Eloheinu Melech haOlam, Pokayach ivrim.

Praised are You YHWH, our Elohim King of the Universe, Who helps the blind to see.

Barukh Atah יהוה, Eloheinu Melech haOlam, Mal'beesh arumim.

Praised are You YHWH, our Elohim King of the Universe, Who clothes the naked.

Barukh Atah יהוה, Eloheinu Melech haOlam, Zokef k'fufim.

Praised are You, YHWH, our Elohim King of the Universe, Who lifts up the fallen.

Barukh Atah יהוה, Eloheinu Melech haOlam, Ha'maychin mitz'aday-gaver.

Praised are You YHWH, our Elohim King of the Universe, Who makes firm our steps.

Barukh Atah יהוה, Eloheinu Melech haOlam, Otayr Yisra'el big'vurah.

Praised are You YHWH, our Elohim King of the Universe, Who girds Yisra'el with strength.

Barukh Atah יהוה, Eloheinu Melech haOlam, Oter Yisra'el b'tif'arah.

Praised are You YHWH, our Elohim King of the Universe, Who crowns Yisra'el with splendor.

Barukh Atah יהוה, Eloheinu Melech haOlam, Hanotayn laya'ayf koach.

Praised are You YHWH, our Elohim King of the Universe, Who gives strength to the weary.

Barukh Atah יהוה, Eloheinu Melech haOlam, Hama'aveer shaynah may'aynai ut numah may'afa'pai.

Praised are You YHWH, our Elohim King of the Universe, Who removes sleep from the eyes, slumber from the eye lids.

MIKRA

The proclamation

Hara'chaman, hu yishtabach l'dor dorim, v'yitpa'ar banu la'ad ul naytzach n'tzchim, v'yit hadar la'ad ul'ol'may olamin. Amein.

May the Merciful One be praised in all generations, be glorified through us to all eternity, and be honoured among us forever. Amein.

Ashreinu!
Ma-tov chelkeinu!
U'ma-na'im goraleinu!
U'ma-yafa yerushateinu!

How greatly we are blessed!
How good is our portion!
How pleasant is our lot!
How beautiful our heritage!

Chazak! Chazak! u'barukh!

Be strong! Be strong and be blessed!

HA-MINCHAH

These are prayers that we make during the afternoon. It is to be recited half an hour after noon time and no later than sunset. Minchan offerings were done during the temple period in the afternoon. See Ahmos (Amos) 5:22 and 5:25. Ha'Minchan means the Afternoon Sacrifices.

TALLIT

The prayer shawl

While holding the Tallit in your hand say:

Barukh Atah יהוה, *Eloheinu Melech haOlam, Asher kidshanu b'mitzvotav v'tzivanu lit'atayf batzitzit.*

Praised are You YHWH, our Elohim King of the Universe, Who sanctified us with Mitzvot, and commands us to wrap ourselves in tzitzit.

TIFILLAT TAMID

The disciple's prayer

Aveinu Shebashamayim yitkadash Sh'mekah.

Our Abba Who is in the shamayim, kadosh shmecha.

Tavo mal'khutekha yay'asay ratzon'kha k'mo bashamayim kayn ba'aretz.

Your malchut come. Your ratzon be done in the earth, as it is in the shamayim.

Et-lechem chukaynu ten-lanu hayom.

Give us today our daily lechem.

Us'lach-lanu et-chovotaynu ka'asher salachnu gam-anachnu lacha-yavanu.

And forgive us our debts, as we forgive our debtors.

Va'al tavee'aynu leeday nisayon ki im-chal'tzaynu min-hara ki l'kah hamamlakha v'hagavura v'hatif'eret l'ol'may olameen. Amein.

And lead us not into temptation, but deliver us from evil: For Yours is the malchut, and the power, and the tifereth, le-olam-va-ed. Amein.

THE TEN REVERSALS

The Beatitudes

Ashray aneeay ruach lahem malakhut hashamayim.

Blessed are the poor in ruach: for theirs is the malchut ha shamayim.

Ashray ha'avaylim ki haym yanuchamu.

Blessed are they that mourn: for they shall be comforted.

Asray ha'anavim ki hayma yiyrshu ha'aretz.

Blessed are the meek: for they shall inherit the Land.

Ashray har'ayvim vahatzmay'im la'tzedakah ki haym yisba'u.

Blessed are they that do hunger and thirst after tzedakah: for they shall be filled.

Ashray ha'rachamanim ki haym yaruchamu.

Blessed are the rachamim givers: for they shall obtain rachamim.
Ashray baray layvav ki haym yechezu et haElohim.

Blessed are the pure in lev: for they shall see Elohim.

Asray rodafee shalom ki banay Elohim yiqaray'u.

Blessed are the shalom-makers: for they shall be called b'nai Elohim.

Ashray hanir'dafim al davar ha'tzedaka ki lahem malkhut hashamayim.

Blessed are those who are persecuted for tzedakah's sake: for theirs is the malchut ha shamayim.

Asharakhem im yicharafu etakhem veedabru vasheker Aleikem kol ra ba'avuree.

Blessed are you, when men shall revile you, and persecute you, and shall say all manner of evil against you falsely, for My sake.

Simachu vageelu ki sakhrakhem rav bashamayim ki khayn radafu et ha'navim asher hainu lifnaykhem.

Gilah, and be in great simcha: for great is your reward in the shamayim: for so persecuted they the nevim who were before you.

BIRKAT HA-SHEM

The blessing of the Name

Barukh haba b'shaym יהוה, *Halleluyah! Amein.*

Praised is He who comes in the name of YHWH, Halleluyah! Amein.

HA-MA'ARIV

These are prayers that we make when retiring in the evening. This is also called the *Birkhot haArvit* meaning the evening blessings and is to be recited anytime between sunset and dawn. It includes the recitation of the *Shema, Hashkiveinu, Aleinu, and Adon Olam*. Ha'Ma'ariv means the Evening Prayer.

TALLIT

The prayer shawl

While holding the Tallit in your hand say:

Barukh Atah יהוה, *Eloheinu Melech haOlam, Asher kidshanu b'mitzvotav v'tzivanu lit'atayf batzitzit.*

Praised are You, YHWH, our Elohim King of the Universe, Who sanctified us with Mitzvot, and commands us to wrap ourselves in tzitzit.

THE SHEMA

The declaration of Yisra'el

Face Yerushalem and say:

Shema Yisra'el יהוה *Eloheinu,* יהוה *Echad!*
(Softly) *Barukh sheim k'vod mal'khuto l'olam va'ed!*

Hear, O Yisra'el: YHWH is our Elohim, the Eternal YHWH alone! (Devarim (Deuteronomy) 6:4) Praised is YHWH's glorious majesty forever and ever!

V'ahavta ayt יהוה *Elohekhah, b'khol l'vav'kha uv'khol nafish'kha uv'khol m'dekha.*

V'hayu had'varim ha'aylay asher anokhee m'tzav'kha hayom al l'vavekha. V'shinantam l'vanekha v'dibarta bam, b'shivt'kha b'vaytekha uvlekht'kha baderekh uv, shokhb'kha uv'kumekha. Uk'shartam l'ot al yadekha v'hayu l'totafot bayn aynekha. Ukh'tavtam al m'zuzot baytekha uvish'arekha. L'ma'an tizk'ru va'asitem et kol mitzvotai Vihyeetem k'doshim laylohaykhem.
Ani יהוה Eloheikhem asher hotzaytee et'khem may'eretz Mitzrayim Lihyot lakhem laylohim.
Ani יהוה Eloheikhem. V'ah havta l'ray kha khamokha. Ani יהוה.

And you shall love YHWH your Elohim with all your lev, and with all your being, and with all your might.
And these words, which I command you this day, shall be in your lev: And you shall teach them diligently to your children, and shall talk of them when you sit in your bayit, and when you walk by the way, and when you lie down, and when you rise up. And you shall bind them for an ot upon your hand, and they shall be as frontlets between your eyes. And you shall write them upon the posts of your bayit, and on your gates. That you may remember, and do all My mitzvoth, and be kadosh to your Elohim.
I am YHWH your Elohim, Who brought you out of the land of Mitzrayim, to be your Elohim: I am YHWH your Elohim.
And you shall love your neighbor as yourself: I am YHWH.

HASHKIVEINU

Declaration of shalom

Hashkiveinu is the second blessing following the Shema during Maariv. It is a petitionary prayer to be able to lie down in peace at night and to return to life the following day.

Hashkivenu, יהוה Eloheinu, l'shalom v'ha'amideinu malkeinu l'chayim. Uf'rosh aleinu sukat sh'lomekha, v'takneinu b'etsa tovah milfanekha, v'hoshi'enu l'ma'an shemekha. V'hagen ba'adenu, v'haser me'aleinu oyev, dever, v'herev, v'ra'av, v'yagon, v'haser satan milfaneinu ume'ach-areinu, uv'tsel k'nafekha tastireinu, ki El shomreinu umatsileinu Atah, ki El Melech chanun v'rachum Atah. Ushmor tsetenu uvo'einu,

l'chayim ul'shalom m'Atah v'ad olam. Ufros aleinu sucat shlomekha.
Barukh Atah, יהוה, *haporeis sukat shalom aleinu, v'al-kol-amo-Yisrael, v'al Yerushalem. Amein.*

Grant O YHWH that we may lie down in peace, and raise us up, O Guardian, to life renewed. Spread over us the shelter of Your peace, guide us with Your good counsel, and for Your Name's sake, be our Help. Blessed are You, YHWH, who spreads a shelter of peace over us, over all the people Yisra'el, and over Yerushalem. Amein.

ALEINU

It is our duty

This pillar among the prayers declares YHWH's sovereignty over all His creation. According to tradition, Yehoshua (Joshua) composed it at the time he crossed the Yarden (Jordan) and entered the Land of Promise. It is generally held, however, that it was first introduced into the daily prayer service by Rav, founder of the Sura Academy (early third century), as an introduction to *Malchuyot*. During the part when we say *"Va'anachnu korim umishtachavim u'modim"* literally "we bow in awe and thanksgiving" we bend the knee and bow while standing.

Aleinu l'shabay-ach la'adon hakol, latayt g'dula l'yotzayr b'raysheet, shelo asanu k'goyay ha'aratzot, velo samanu k'mishp'chot ha'adamah; shelo sam chelkaynu kahem, v'goraleinu k'chol hamonam.
Va'anachnu korim umishtachavim u'modim lif'nay Melech mal'khay Ham'lakhim, hakodosh Barukh Hu.

We must praise the Elohim of all, the maker of heaven and Earth, Who has set us apart from the other families of the Earth, giving us a destiny unique among the nations.
Therefore we bow in awe and thanksgiving before the One Who is Sovereign over all, the Set Apart Blessed One.

Shehu notay shamayim v'yosayd aretz umoshav y'karo bashamayim mima'al, ush'chinat zob'gov'haym'romim.
Hu Eloheinu ayn nod. Emet malkaynu efes zulato, kakatuv b'torato "V'yada'ta hayom v'hashayvota El- l'vave'kha, ki יהוה hu ha'Elohim bashamayim mima'al v'al ha aretz mitachat, ayn nod" Kakatuv b'torahte'kha. יהוה yimloch l'olam va'ed. V'ne'emar: v'hayah יהוה yimloach l'Melech al kol ha'aretz; bayom hahu yihyeh יהוה echad, ush'mo echad!

You stretch out the heavens and the establish the Earth (Yeshayahu (Isaiah) 51:13);
You are our Elohim; there is none else. In truth You alone are our Sovereign Elohim, as it is written: "Know this day and take it to heart; YHWH is Elohim in the heavens above and on the Earth below; there is none else" (Devarim (Deuteronomy) 4:39).
And it has been said; YHWH shall rule over all the Earth; as it is written in your Torah. YHWH shall reign for all eternity. On that day YHWH shall be One and Your name shall be One (Zecharyah (Zechariah) 14:9).

ADON OLAM

The Eternal Master of the Universe

Adon Olam "Eternal Master" or "Infinite Master" is a strictly metrical hymn in the Jewish liturgy. It has been a regular part of the daily and Sabbath liturgy since the 15th century. Its authorship and origin are uncertain. Although its diction indicates antiquity, it did not become part of the prayer liturgy until the 15th century. This song is sung to many different tunes, and can be sung to virtually any tune.

Adon Olam, asher malach b'terem kol-y'tzir niv'ra, l'eit na'asah v'cheftzo kol, azai Melech sh'mo nikra.
V'acharei kich'lot hakol, l'vado yimloch nora; v'hu hayah, v'hu hoveh, v'hu yih'yeh b'tif'arah.
V'hu echad, v'ein sheini l'hamshil lo, l'hach'bira, bli reisheet, b'li tach'lit, v'lo ha'oz v'hamis'ra.

V'hu Eili, v'chai go'ali, v'tzir chev'li v'eit tzara, V'hu nisi umanos li, m'nat kosi b'yom ek'ra.
B'yado af'kid ruchi, b'eit ishan v'aira, V'im ruchi g'viyati, Adonai li, v'lo ira.

You are the Eternal Master of the Universe, Who reigned before any being had been created; when all was done according to Your will, already then You were Sovereign. And after all has ceased to be, still You reign in solitary majesty; You were, You are, You will be in esteem. And You are One; none other can compare to You, or consort with You; You are without beginning, without end; You alone are power and dominion. And You are my Elohim, my living Redeemer, my Rock in time of trouble and distress; You are my banner and my refuge, my benefactor when I call on You. Into Your hands I entrust my spirit, when I sleep and when I wake; and with my spirit, my body also: My Master is with me, I shall not fear.

Y'hiyu l'ratzon im'rei fi v'hegyon libi l'fanekha, יהוה tzuri v'goali. Amein.

May the words of my mouth and the meditation of my lev be acceptable to You, O YHWH, my Rock and my Redeemer. Amein. (Tehillim (Psalm) 19:14).

MA-TOVU

Ma Tovu literally "O How Good" or "How Goodly" is a prayer expressing reverence and awe for Synagogues and other places of worship. It can be applied to a home where YHWH is being reverenced. It is usually recited upon entering the Synagogue or the place. The prayer starts with Bamidbar (Numbers) 24:5, where Balaam, sent to curse the Israelites, is instead overcome with awe at YHWH and the Israelites Tabernacle of worship. Its first line of praise is a quote of Balaam's blessing. The remainder of the text is derived from passages in Tehillim (Psalms) relating to entering the house of worship and preparation for further prayer (Tehillim (Psalms) 5:8; 26:8; 95:6; and 69:14).

MA TOVU

O how good

Ma tovu ohalekha Ya'akov, mishk'notekha Yisra'el. Va'ani b'rov hasd'kha, avo veytekha,
Eshtahaveh el heikhal kodsh'kha b'yir'atekha. יהוה *ahavti m'on beitekha, um-kom mishkan k'vodekha. Va'ani eshtahave v'ekhra'a. Evr'kha lifnei Adonai osi.*
Va'ani t'filati l'kha יהוה *et ratzon. Elohim b'rov hasdekha aneini b'emet yish'ekha.*

How lovely are your tents, O Ya'akov, your dwelling-places, O Yisra'el! In your abundant loving kindness, O YHWH, I enter Your Tabernacle, reverently to worship in awe in Your Set Apart House. Master, I love Your Tabernacle, the place where Your presence dwells. So I would worship with humility, I would seek blessing in the presence of Adonai, my maker. To You, then, YHWH, does my prayer go forth. May this be a time of joy and favour. In Your great love, O Elohim, answer me with Your saving truth.

HALELU B'SHAYM

It is the solemn duty of every emet follower (Tzadik) of YHWH to praise the Name of YHWH. Both the TaNaK and Brit Chadashah teach that it is the responsibility of the Tzadik to praise His Name daily. Consider the following of which are only a few examples;

"*At that time* יהוה *separated the tribe of Lewi, to bear the Ark of the Testimony of* יהוה, *to stand before* יהוה *to attend to Him, and to bless in His Name, to this day*" Devarim (Deuteronomy) 10:8.

"*Give hodu (praise) to* יהוה, *call upon His Name make known His deeds among the nations.*" Divre Hayamim Alef (First Chronicles) 16:8.

"*The sons of Amram; Aharon and Moshe; and Aharon was separated, that he should sanctify the most kadosh (set apart) things, he and his sons le-olam-va-ed, to burn incense before* יהוה; *to attend to Him, and to bless in His Name le-olam-va-ed (forever)*" Divre Hayamim Alef (First Chronicles) 23:13.

"*And in that day shall you say, BARUCH HA-SHEM* יהוה, *(Bless The Name) call upon His Name, declare His doings among the nations, make mention that His Name is exalted*" Yeshayahu (Isaiah) 12:4.

"*Give to* יהוה, *O you sons of the mighty, give to* יהוה *tifereth (esteem) and strength. Give to* יהוה *the tifereth (esteem) due to His Name; worship* יהוה *in the beauty of set-apartness*" Tehillim (Psalms) 29:1-2.

"*Sing forth the honor of His Name; make His hallel (praise) beautiful*" Tehillim (Psalms) 66:2.

"Sing to Elohim, shir tehillot (praises) to His Name: extol Him that rides upon the shamayim by His Name YAH, and gilah (rejoice) before Him" Tehillim (Psalms) 68:4.

"I will hallel (praise) the Name of Elohim with a shir (song), and will magnify Him with hodu (thanksgiving)" Tehillim (Psalms) 69:30.

"Give to יהוה the tifereth (esteem) due to His Name: bring an offering, and come into His courts. O worship יהוה in the beauty of set-apartness: fear Him, all the earth" Tehillim (Psalms) 96:8.

"Hallel (praise) יהוה; for יהוה is tov (good): shir tehillot (sing praises) to His Name; for it is pleasant" Tehillim (Psalms) 135:3.

"Let them hallel (praise) the Name of יהוה: for His Name alone is excellent; His tifereth (esteem) is above the earth and the shamayim (heaven). O magnify יהוה with me, and let us exalt His Name together" Tehillim (Psalms) 148:13.

"Let them hallel (praise) His Name in the dance: let them shir tehillot (sing praises) to Him with the tambourine and harp" Tehillim (Psalms) 149:3.

"By Him therefore let us offer the sacrifice of tehilla (praise) to יהוה continually, that is, the fruit of our lips giving hodu (thanks) to His Name" Ivrim (Hebrews) 13:15.

What follows is a *Tefillot Kohanim* (Priestly prayer) for praising the great Name of YHWH.

BIRKAT SHEM GADOL

The blessing of the Great Name

Face Yerushalem and say:

Barukh Atah יהוה, Eloheinu Melech haOlam, Asher kidshanu b'mitzvotav v'tzivanu, Halelu b'Shaym.

Praised are You YHWH, our Elohim King of the Universe, Who sanctified us with Mitzvot, and commands us to Praise His Name.

Adonai, s'fatai tifach, ufee yageed, t'hilatekah.

Sovereign Elohim open my lips, that my mouth may declare Your esteem.

Aleinu l'shabay-ach la'adon hakol, latayt g'dula l'yotzayr b'raysheet, shelo asanu k'goyay ha'aratzot, velo samanu k'mishp'chot ha'adamah; shelo sam chelkaynu kahem, v'goraleinu k'chol hamonam.
Va'anachnu korim umishtachavim u'modim lif'nay Melech mal'khay Ham'lakhim, hakodosh Barukh Hu.

We must praise the Elohim of all, the maker of heaven and earth, Who has set us apart from the other families of the Earth, giving us a destiny unique among the nations. Therefore we bow in awe and thanksgiving before the One Who is Sovereign over all, the Holy Blessed One.

Mi Chamokhah ba'aylim יהוה
Mi Chamokhah ne'dar bakodesh nora t'hilot osay felay.

Who is like You, among the gods, YHWH.
Who is like You set part from all, awesome in praises, doing wanders.

Shehu notay shamayim v'yosayd aretz umoshav y'karo bashamayim mima'al, ush'chinat zob'gov'haym'romim. Hu Eloheinu ayn nod. Emet malkaynu efes zulato, kakatuv b'torato "V'yada'ta hayom v'hashayvota El- l'vave'kha, ki יהוה hu ha'Elohim bashamayim mima'al v'al ha aretz mitachat, ayn nod" Kakatuv b'torahte'kha. יהוה yimloch l'olam va'ed. V'ne'emar: v'hayah יהוה yimloach l'Melech al kol ha'aretz; bayom hahu yihyeh יהוה echad, ush'mo echad!

"You stretched forth the shamayim, and laid the foundations of the Earth" (Yeshayahu (Isaiah) 51:13); You are our Elohim; there is none else. In truth You alone are our Sovereign Elohim, as it is written: *"Know therefore this day, and consider it in your lev, that* יהוה *He is Elohim in the shamayim above, and upon the earth beneath: there is none else"* (Devarim (Deuteronomy) 4:39. And it has been said; *"And* יהוה *shall be Melech over all the earth: in that day shall there be* יהוה *echad, and His Name echad"* Zecharyah (Zechariah) 14:9).

Mal'kut'khara'u vanekha, bokay'a yam lif'nay Moshay; "Zay ayli!" "anu v'am'ru; יהוה *yimlokh l'olam va'ed!"*

Your children saw your sovereign might displayed as you split the sea before Moshe. *"This is my Elohim"* they cried. *"* יהוה *shall reign le-olam-va-ed!"* Shemoth (Exodus) 15:2, 18.

V'ne'emar: ki-fadah יהוה *et-Ya'akov ug'alo miyad Chazak mimenu. Barukh Atah,* יהוה *ga'al Yisra'el.*

And it has been said; *"For* יהוה *has redeemed Yaakov, and ransomed him from the hand of him that was stronger than he."* Yirmeyahu (Jeremiah) 31:11.

Praised is YHWH, Redeemer of Yisra'el.

Y'hay sh'meih raba m'vorach l'olam ul'al'may al'ma-ya. Yitbarakh v'yishtabach v'yitpa'ar v'yitronmam v'yitnasay v'yithadar v'yit'aleh v'yit'halel sh'meih d'kud'sha, b'reekh hu,

L'ayla min kol bir'khata v'sheerata tush'b'chata v'nechemata da'ameern b'alma v'imru. Amein.

L'ayla min kol bir'khata, v'sheerata, tush' b'chata v'nechemata da'ameeran b'alma v'imru, Amein.

Lets Elohim's great Name be praise forever and ever. Beyond all praises, songs and adorations that we can utter is the Set Apart One, the Blessed One, Whom we magnify, honour and exalt. And let us say Amein.
Beyond, all blessings, hymns, adoration, and praises, which are uttered in the Universe, and they shall say Amein.

Gad'lu La Adonai itee,un'rom'mah sh'mo yachdav.

Proclaim the greatness of Elohim with me, and let us elevate Elohim's Name together (Tehillim (Psalm) 34:4).

1. *Barukh Atah יהוה El Shaddai magayn Avraham v'ezrat Sarah.*

Praised are You YHWH the all Powerful Mighty One, Shield of Avraham, Protector of Sarah.

2. *Barukh Atah יהוה Elyon, Ha'El hakadosh.*

Praised are You YHWH the Most High Mighty One, Who is Set Apart.

3. *Barukh Atah יהוה El Olam, Shehakol nihya bid'varo.*

Praised are You YHWH, the Mighty One of Eternity, Whose Word caused everything to be.

4. *Barukh Atah יהוה El Dauth, Shekocho ug'vurato malay Olam.*

Praise are You YHWH the Mighty One of Knowledge, Whose power and might fill the World.

5. *Barukh Atah יהוה Mekadishkhem, chonayn hada'at.*

Praised are You YHWH our Sanctification, gracious Giver of knowledge.

6. *Barukh Atah* יהוה *El Gibor, Zokhayr hab'reet v'ne'eman biv'reeto v'kaiyom b'ma'amaro.*

Praised are You YHWH our Mighty Elohim, Who remembers His Covenant and is faithful to His covenant and fulfils His Word.

7. *Barukh Atah* יהוה *Tzemach, Matzmeeach keren yeshua.*

Praised are You YHWH the Branch, Who causes the light of salvation to dawn for all the world.

8. *Barukh Atah* יהוה *Yehoshua, M'cha-yay hamaytim.*

Praised are You YHWH Our Saviour, Who resurrects the dead.

9. *Barukh Atah* יהוה *Avinu, Harotzeh bitshuvah.*

Praised are You YHWH Our Father, Who delights in repentance.

10. *Barukh Atah* יהוה *Rhoi, Chanun hamarbeh lisloach.*

Praised are You YHWH Our Shepherd, Who is merciful and always ready to forgive.

11. *Barukh Atah* יהוה *Ropheka, cholay amo Yisra'el.*

Praised are you YHWH our Healer, Healer of the sick of His people Yisra'el.

12. *Barukh Atah* יהוה *Shaphat, ohayv tz'dakah u'misphat.*

Praised are You YHWH our Supreme Judge, Who loves righteousness and justice.

13. *Barukh Atah* יהוה *Tseba'ot, Mish'an umiv'tach la'tzadikim.*

Praised are You YHWH of Hosts, Staff and Support of the righteous.

14. *Barukh Atah* יהוה *Melech, She'ot'kha l'vad'kha b'yir'ah na'avod.*

Praised are You YHWH our King, Whom alone we serve.

15. *Barukh Atah* יהוה *Tzidkenu, Goayl Yisra'el.*

Praised are you YHWH of Our Righteousness, Redeemer of Yisra'el.

16. *Barukh Atah* יהוה *Nissi, m'kabaytz nid'chay amo Yisra'el.*

Praised are You YHWH Our Banner, Who gathers the dispersed of Your people Yisra'el.

17. *Barukh Atah* יהוה *Yireh, M'varaykh hashanim.*

Praised are you YHWH our Provider, for You bless earth's seasons from year to year.

18. *Barukh Atah* יהוה *Shammah, haTov v'hamayteev.*

Praised are You YHWH Who is there, Who is Good and does good.

19. *Barukh Atah* יהוה *Tzur, Dayan haEmet.*

Praised are You YHWH our Rock, Who is Judge of truth.

20. *Barukh Atah* יהוה *Shalom Asah, Boneh Yerushalem.*

Praised are You YHWH Maker of Peace, Builder of Yerushalem.

21. *Barukh Atah* יהוה *El Roi, Shomayh tifilah.*

Praised are You YHWH the All Seeing Elohim, Who hearkens to prayer.

יהוה *Kadosh, Kadosh, Kadosh!*

YHWH Kadosh, Kadosh, Kadosh!

יהוה *Ensof m'lokhol haAretz k'vodo. Ha'Ribbono shel Olam.*

YHWH Eternal; all the Earth is full of His esteem. The Master of the Universe.

Va'anachnu n'varaykh ya may'Atah v'ad olam Hal'luyah.
Kol han'shama t'halel Yah Hal'luyah.

We shall bless Elohim now and forever Halleluyah! (Tehillim (Palm) 115:18).

Let every soul praise Yah. Halleluyah! (Tehillim (Psalm) 150).

L'kha יהוה*, hag'dulah v'hag'vurah v'hatif'eret v'hanaytzakh v'hahod, kee khol bashamayim uva'aretz, l'kha* יהוה *hamamlakha v'hamitnasay l'khol l'rosh.*

Yours, O YHWH is the greatness, the power, the esteem, the victory and the majesty: for all that is in heaven and earth is Yours. You, O YHWH are Sovereign; You are supreme overall.

V'ayra'teekh lee l'olam, V'ayra'teekh lee b'tzadek uv'mispat uv'chesaid uv'rachameem, V'ayras'teekh lee be'emuna vayada'at et יהוה*.*

I will wed You to me forever. I will wed You to me with right and justice, with love and mercy. I will wed You to me with faith and you shall know YHWH.

Barahu, et יהוה *hameevorakh. Barukh* יהוה *hameevorakh l'olam va'ed.*

Praise YHWH Who is to be praised. Praised is YHWH Who is to be praised forever and ever.

Sing or read this part:

Shema Yisra'el יהוה Eloheinu, יהוה Echad!
(Softly) *Barukh sheim k'vod mal'khuto l'olam va'ed!*

Hear, O Yisra'el: YHWH is our Elohim, the Eternal YHWH alone! (Devarim (Deuteronomy) 6:4) Praised is YHWH's glorious majesty forever and ever!

Declare this seven times:

Echad Eloheinu gadol יהוה kadosh sh'mo.

Our Elohim is One, great is our Sovereign YHWH Awesome is His Name.

Declare this once:

Barukh יהוה Ham vorakh l'olam va'ed!

Praised be YHWH to Whom our praise is due, now and forever!

Barukh shem k'vod Malkhuto l'olam va'ed. Amein.

Praised is the name of His mighty Kingdom forever and ever. Amein.

MIKRA-YERUSHALEM

Mikra is the Hebrew word for proclamation. In the TaNaK we are commanded to make proclamations. One of those important things we are to make proclamations for is the Peace of Yerushalem. We call this type of prayer *Torah Tellifah*. Torah Tefillah transcends every tradition of prayer because it is outside the scope of human deed and human sacrifice because its foundation is not manmade or man centred. It emanates direct from Elohim (the Creator) having the full endorsement and sanction of Heaven because it is proclamming His written Word. The Word of YHWH does not return unfulfilled. It will always accomplish that in which it is sent to do, regardless of the mediator, their conditions or circumstances. It is guranteeed by His Word.

"For as the rain comes down, and the snow from the shamayim (heaven), and returns not there, but waters the earth, and makes it bring forth and bud, that it may give zera (seed) to the sower, and lechem (bread) to the eater: **So shall My Word be that goes forth out of My mouth: it shall not return to Me void, but it shall accomplish that which I please, and it shall prosper in the thing where I send it"** Yeshayahu (Isaiah) 55:10-11.

Let us proclaim together the promises of YHWH for Yerushalem.

MIKRA YERUSHALEM

Proclamation for Yerushalem

Face Yerushalem and say:

Barukh Atah, יהוה *Eloheinu, Melekh haOlam, Asher kid'shanu b'mitzvotav v'tzivanu al Mitzvah t'fillot shaalu shalom Yerushalem.*

Praised are You, YHWH, our Elohim, King of the Universe, Who sanctified us with Mitzvot and has commanded us to pray for the peace of Yerushalem.

"For יהוה will not forsake His people for His great Name's sake: because it has pleased יהוה to make you His people (Yisra'el)" Schmuel Alef (First Samuel) 12:22.

"Save Your people, and bless Your inheritance: feed them also, and lift them up le-olam-va-ed (forever)" Tehillim (Psalms) 28:9.

"Do tov (good) in Your tov pleasure to Tzion (Zion): rebuild the walls of Yahrushalayim (Yerushalem)" Tehillim (Psalms) 51:18.

"Yahrushalayim (Yerushalem) is built as a city that is compact together: Where the tribes go up, the tribes of Yah, to the testimony of Yisrael, to give hodu (thanks) to the Name of יהוה. For there are the set thrones of mishpat (judgment), the thrones of Beit Dawid (House of David). Shaalu shalom Yahrushalayim (pray for the peace of Yerushalem): they shall prosper that love You. Shalom (peace) be within your walls, and prosperity within your citadels. For my brothers and companions' sakes, I will now say, Shalom be within you. Because of the Bayit (House) of יהוה our Elohim I will seek your tov (good)" Tehillim (Psalms) 122:3-9.

"If it had not been יהוה who was on our side, when men rose up against us: Then they would have swallowed us up quickly, when their anger was lit against us: Then the mayim (water) would have overwhelmed us, the stream would have gone over our being: Then the proud mayim (water) would have gone over our being. Blessed be יהוה, who has not given us as a prey to their teeth. Our being has escaped as a bird out of the trap of the bird hunters: the trap is broken, and we have escaped. Our help is in the Name of יהוה, who made the shamayim (heavens) and earth" Tehillim (Psalms) 124:2-8.

"As the mountains are all around Yahrushalayim (Yerushalem), so יהוה is all around His people, from this time forward and even

le-olam-va-ed (forever). For the rod of the wicked shall not rest upon the lot of the tzadikim (Yisrael); lest the tzadikim (righteous) put forth their hands to iniquity" Tehillim (Psalms) 125.

"Your shoes (Yahrushalayim) shall be iron and brass; and as your days, so shall your strength be. There is none like the El (Creator) of Yeshurun, who rides upon the shamayim (heavens) to help you, and in His excellency rides the skies. The Elohim of old is your refuge, and underneath are the everlasting arms: and He shall thrust out the enemy from before you; and shall say, Destroy them. Yisrael then shall dwell in safety alone: the fountain of Yaakov (Jacob) shall be upon a land of corn and wine; also His shamayim (heavens) shall drop down dew. Favored are you, O Yisrael: who is like you, O people saved by יהוה, the Shield of your help, who is the Sword of Your Excellency! And your enemies shall be found to be liars to you; and you shall tread down their high place." Devarim (Deuteronomy) 33:25-29.

"יהוה builds up Yahrushalayim (Yerushalem): He gathers together the outcasts of Yisrael" Tehillim (Psalms) 147:2.

"And it shall come to pass in that day, that the great shofar (rams horn) shall be blown, and they shall come who were ready to perish in the land of Ashshur, and the outcasts in the land of Mitzrayim (Egypt), and shall worship יהוה in the kadosh (set apart) mountain at Yahrushalayim (Yerushalem)" Yeshayahu (Isaiah) 27:13.

"And I will restore your shophtim (judges) as at the first, and your counselors as at the beginning: afterward you shall be called, The city of tzedakah, (righteous) the faithful city. Tzion (Zion) shall be redeemed with mishpat (judgment), and her restored ones with tzedakah (righteous)" Yeshayahu (Isaiah) 1:26-27.

"And it shall come to pass in the yamim acharonim (the age of the Messiah), that the mountain of יהוה's Bayit (House) shall be established on the top of the mountains, and shall be exalted above the hills; and all nations shall flow to it. And many nations

shall go and say, Come, and let us make aliyah (return) to the mountain of יהוה, *to the Bayit (House) of the Elohim of Yaakov (Jacob); and He will teach us His halachot (ways), and we will have our halacha (path) in His paths: for out of Tzion (Zion) shall go forth the Torah, and the word of* יהוה *from Yahrushalayim (Yerushalem). And He shall be a shofet (judge) between the nations, and shall rebuke many peoples: and they shall beat their swords into plowshares, and their spears into pruning hooks: nation shall not lift up sword against nation, neither shall they learn war any more"* Yeshayahu (Isaiah) 2:2-4.

"For the people shall live in Tzion (Zion) at Yahrushalayim (Yerushalem): you shall weep no more: He will have great rachamim (mercy) towards you at the voice of your cry; when He shall hear, He will answer you" Yeshayahu (Isaiah) 30:19.

"For this has יהוה *spoken to me, Like as the lion and the young lion roaring on its prey, when a multitude of shepherds is called forth against him, he will not be afraid of their voice, nor humble himself for the noise of them: so shall* יהוה *tzevaoth (Hosts) come down to fight for Har Tzion (Zion), and for its hill. As birds flying, so will* יהוה *tzevaoth (Hosts) defend Yahrushalayim (Yerushalem); defending and delivering it; and passing over and preserving it"* Yeshayahu (Isaiah) 31:4-5.

"Look upon Tzion (Zion), the city of our moadim (feasts): Your eyes shall see Yahrushalayim (Yerushalem) a quiet home, a sukkah (Tabernacle) that shall not be taken down; not one of its pegs shall ever be removed, neither shall any of its cords be broken. But there Majestic יהוה *will be to us a place of broad rivers and streams; in which shall go no boat with oars, neither shall large ships pass by. For* יהוה *is our Shofet (Judge),* יהוה *is our Torah-Giver,* יהוה *is our Melech (the King); He will save us"* Yeshayahu (Isaiah) 33:20-22.

"Nachamu, Nachamu Ami-My people (comfort yes comfort my people), says your Elohim (Creator). Speak comfortably to Yahrushalayim (Yerushalem), and declare to her, that her warfare is finished, that her iniquity is pardoned: for she has received

from יהוה's hand double for all her sins. The voice of him that cries in the wilderness, Prepare the Way of יהוה, make straight in the desert a derech (highway) for our Elohim. Every valley shall be exalted, and every mountain and hill shall be made low: and the crooked places shall be made straight, and the rough places plain: And the tifereth (esteem) of יהוה shall be revealed, and all flesh shall see it together: for the mouth of יהוה has spoken it. The voice said, Cry. And he said, What shall I cry? All flesh is grass, and all the tov (good) from it is as the flower of the field: The grass withers, the flower fades: when the Ruach Hakodesh (the Set Apart Spirit) of יהוה blows upon it: surely the people are like grass. The grass withers, the flower fades: but the word of our Elohim (Creator) shall abide and stand le-olam-va-ed (forever). O Tzion (Zion), that brings tov tidings, get up into the high mountain; O Yahrushalayim (Yerushalem), that brings tov (good) tidings, lift up your voice with strength; lift it up, be not afraid; say to the cities of Yahudah (Judah), See your Elohim" Yeshayahu (Isaiah) 40:1-9.

Hara'chaman, hu yislach lanu et-Eliyahu Hanavi, zakhur latov, veevaser-lanu b'sorot tovot y'shuot v'nechamot.

May the merciful One send Eliyahu the Prophet to us, and me he bear good tidings of salvation and comfort.

Uv'nay Yerushalem eer hakodesh bimheira v'yamaynu.
Barukh Atah יהוה beneh, v'rachamav Yerushalem with mercy. Amein.

May Elohim rebuild Yerushalem, the Set Apart City, speedily in our lifetime.

Praised is YHWH, Who restores Yerushalem with mercy. Amein.

MIKRA-YISRA'EL

Mikra is the Hebrew word for proclamation. In the TaNaK we are commanded to make proclamations. One of those important things we are to make proclamations for is for the restoration of Yisra'el. During the period of 745-721 B.C. the 10 Northern tribes were exiled by King Tilgat Pilsger 111 to Assyria and then to lands beyond the Euphrates where they were eventually driven to the four corners of the Earth as Moshe had prophesied (Devarim (Deuteronomy) 4:26; 28:64).

The prophecy of Yechezkel (Ezekiel) 4:4-5 shows that they were to be punished for 390 years for worshiping Baal/Asherap. Having not repented after 390 years in captivity, the Northern tribes then had to endure the seven fold increase of the penalty according to Wayiqra (Leviticus) 26:27, 28 (70 X 390 years from 721 B.C). That means they would be in exile for another 2730 years. Using the perpetual Hebrew Calendar this period formally ended in 2008.

It means that Ephraim's period of prolonged captivity is over! YHWH will once again extend His mercy, love and compassion to Ephraim, recover and rejoin the 10 tribes to Yisra'el (Yeshayahu (Isaiah) 11:11-14; 27:9, Yirmeyahu (Jeremiah) 3:14-18, 16:11-16, 50:4-5, 20, Yechezkel (Ezekiel) 37:22-26, Zecharyah (Zechariah) 8:3, 7, 13:9; 13:10, 7, 8, 10 Hoshea (Hosea) 1:11, Ovadyah (Obadiah) 1:18, Schmuel Alef (First Samuel) 17:45).

Let us proclaim together the promises of YHWH for Yisra'el.

MIKRA YISRA'EL

Proclammation for Yisra'el

Face Yerushalem and say:

Barukh Atah, יהוה Eloheinu, Melekh haOlam, Asher kid'shanu b'mitzvotav v'tzivanu al Mitzvah t'fillot v'al boneh v'rachamav Yisrael.
Barukh Atah יהוה goayl Yisra'el.

Praised are You, YHWH, our Elohim, King of the Universe, Who sanctified us with Mitzvot and has commanded us to pray for the restoration of Yisrael.
We praise you, O YHWH, Redeemer of Yisra'el.

"Then shall you cause the shofar (rams horn) of the yovel (Jubilee) to sound on the tenth day of the seventh month, on the Yom HaKippurim (feast of Atonement) shall you make the shofar (rams horn) sound throughout all your land. And you shall set-apart the fiftieth year, and proclaim liberty throughout all the land to all the inhabitants of it: it shall be a yovel (Jubilee) to you; and you shall return every man to his possession, and you shall return every man to his mishpacha (family). A yovel (Jubilee) shall that fiftieth year be to you: you shall not sow; neither reap that which grows by itself in it, nor gather the grapes in it of your undressed vine. For it is the yovel (Jubilee); it shall be kadosh (set apart) to you: you shall eat the increase of it out of the field. In the year of this yovel (Jubilee) you shall return every man to his possession. And if you sell some item to your neighbor, or buy from your neighbor's hand, you shall not oppress one another" Wayiqra (Leviticus) 24:9-14.

"At the end of every seven years you shall make a release. And this is the manner of the release: Every creditor that lends anything to his neighbor shall release it; he shall not require it from his neighbor, or from his brother; because it is called יהוה 's release. From a foreigner you may exact it again: but that which is yours with your brother your hand shall release; There shall be

no poor among you; for יהוה *shall greatly bless you in the land which* יהוה *your Elohim gives you for an inheritance to possess"* Devarim (Deuteronomy) 15:1-4.

"And afterward Moshe and Aharon went in, and told Pharaoh, this says יהוה *Elohim of Yisrael, Let My people go, that they may hold a moed (feast) to Me in the wilderness"* Shemoth (Exodus) 5:1

"For this has יהוה *said to me, Go, set a watchman, and let him declare what he sees. And he cried, A lion: my master, I stand continually upon the watchtower in the daytime, and I am set in my post every night: And, see, here comes a mirkavah (chariot) of men, with a couple of horsemen. And he answered and said, Bavel is fallen, it is fallen; and all the graven images of her elohim He has broken to the ground"* Yeshayahu (Isaiah) 21:6-9.

"That then יהוה *your Elohim will turn your captivity, and have compassion upon you, and will return and gather you from all the nations, where* יהוה *your Elohim has scattered you. 4 If any of you are driven out to the farthest parts of the shamayim (heavens), from there will* יהוה *your Elohim gather you, and from there will He fetch you"* Devarim (Deuteronomy) 30:3-4.

"But, יהוה *lives, that brought up the children of Yisrael from the land of the north, and from all the lands where He had driven them: and I will bring them again into their land that I gave to their ahvot (forefathers). See, I will send for many fishers, says* יהוה *and they shall fish them; and after that will I send for many hunters, and they shall hunt them from every mountain, and from every hill, and out of the holes of the rocks. For My eyes are upon all their derachot (pathways): they are not hidden from My face, neither is their iniquity hidden from My eyes"* Yirmeyahu (Jeremiah) 16:15-17.

"The remnant shall return, even the remnant of Yaakov (Jacob), to the Mighty-El. For though your people O Yisrael be as the sand of the sea, yet a remnant of them shall return: their numbers

decreased yet overflowing with tzedakah (righteousness)" Yeshayahu (Isaiah) 43:21-22.

"Since you were precious in My sight, you have been honorable, and I have loved you: therefore will I give men for you, and people for your chayim (life). Fear not: for I am with you: I will bring your zera (seed) from the east, and gather you from the west; I will say to the north, Give them up; and to the south, keep them not back: bring My sons from far, and My daughters from the ends of the earth" Yeshayahu (Isaiah) 43:4-6.

"He brought them out of darkness and the shadow of death, and broke their chains in pieces. Oh that men would hallel (praise) יהוה for His tov (good), and for His wonderful works to the children of men!" Tehillim (Psalms) 107:14-15.

"Fear not; for you shall not be ashamed: neither will you be embarrassed; for you shall not be put to shame: for you shall forget the shame of your youth, and shall not remember the reproach of your widowhood any more. For your Maker is your Husbands יהוה tzevaoth (of hosts) is His Name; and your Redeemers the Kadosh-One of Yisrael (set apart); The Elohim of the whole earth shall He be called. For יהוה has called you back as a woman forsaken and grieved in ruach (spirit), like a wife of youth, when you were refused, says your Elohim. For a small moment have I forsaken you; but with great rachamim (mercy) will I gather you. In an overflow of My wrath I hid My face from you for a moment; but with everlasting chesed (favour) will I have rachamim (mercy) on you, says יהוה your Redeemer. For this is as the mayim (water) of Noach to Me: for as I have sworn that the mayim (water) of Noach should no more go over the earth; so have I sworn that I would not be angry with you, nor rebuke you again. For the mountains shall depart, and the hills shall be removed; but My chesed (favour) shall not depart from you again, neither shall the brit (covenant) of My shalom (peace) be removed, says יהוה that has rachamim (mercy) on you" Yeshayahu (Isaiah) 54:4-10.

"Therefore say, this says the Master יהוה *; I will even gather you from the peoples, and assemble you out of the countries where you have been scattered, and I will give you the land of Yisrael. And they shall come to the land, and they shall take away all the detestable things of the land and all the abominations from there. And I will give them lev echad (one heart), and I will put a new Ruach (Spirit) inside you; and I will take the stony lev (heart) out of their flesh, and will give them a lev (heart) of flesh: That they may have their halacha (pathway) in My chukim (statutes) and keep My mishpatim (judgements), and do them: and they shall be My people-Ami, and I will be their Elohim"* Yechezkel (Ezekiel) 11:17-20.

"See, the days are coming, says יהוה*, that I will make a Brit Chadasha-Renewed Brit with Beit Yisrael (house of Israel), and with Beit Yahudah (house of Judah): Not according to the brit (covenant) that I made with their ahvot (forefathers) in the day that I took them by the hand to bring them out of the land of Mitzrayim (Egypt); which brit (covenant) they broke, although I was a husband to them, says* יהוה *: But this shall be the brit that I will make with Beit Yisrael (house of Israel), after those days, says* יהוה*, I will put My Torah in their inward parts, and write it on their levim (hearts); and will be their Elohim, and they shall be My People-Ami. And they shall teach no more every man his neighbor, and every man his brother, saying, Know* יהוה*: for they shall all know Me, from the least of them to the greatest of them, says* יהוה*; for I will forgive their iniquity, and I will remember their sin no more"* Yirmeyahu (Jeremiah) 31:31-34.

"For I will take you out from among the gentiles, and gather you out of all countries, and will bring you into your own land. Then will I sprinkle clean mayim (water) upon you, and you shall be clean: from all your filthiness, and from all your idols, will I cleanse you. A new lev (heart) also will I give you, and a new Ruach (Spirit) will I put inside you: and I will take away the stony lev (heart) out of your flesh, and I will give you a lev (heart) of flesh. And I will put My Ruach Hakodesh (the Setapart Spirit) inside you, and cause you to have a halacha (pathways) in My chukim (Statues), and you shall guard My mishpatim (judgments),

and do them. And you shall dwell in the land that I gave to your ahvot (fathers); and you shall be My people-Ami, and I will be your Elohim" Yechezkel (Ezekiel) 36:24-28.

"And the word of יהוה *came to me, saying, Ben-adam (Son of Adam), prophesy against the shepherds of Yisrael, prophesy, and say to them, This says the Master* יהוה *to the shepherds; Woe to the shepherds of Yisrael that do feed themselves! Should not the shepherds feed the flocks? You eat the fat, and you clothe yourself with wool, you where they have been scattered in the cloudy and dark day. And I will bring them out from the nations, and gather them from the countries, and will bring them to their own land, and feed them upon the mountains of Yisrael by the rivers, and in all the inhabited places of the country. I will feed them in a tov (good) pasture, and upon the high mountains of Yisrael shall their fold be: there shall they lie down in a tov (good) fold, and in a fat pasture shall they feed upon the mountains of Yisrael. I will feed My flock, and I will cause them to lie down, says the Master* יהוה*. I will seek that which was lost, and bring again that which was driven away, and will bind up that which was broken, and will strengthen that which was sick: but I will destroy the fat and the strong; I will feed them with mishpat (judgement)"* Yechezkel (Ezekiel) 34:1-7.

"For the Ben Ahdahm (son of Adam) has come to save that which was lost" Mattityahu (Matthew) 18:11.

"He that is not with Me is against Me; and he that gathers not with Me scatters abroad" Mattityahu (Matthew) 12:30.

"But He answered and said, they did not send Me but to the lost sheep of Beit Yisrael (house of Israel), who went astray" Mattityahu (Matthew) 15:24.

"These twelve Yeshua sent forth, and commanded them, saying, Go not the way of the gentiles by staying away from pagan practices, and into any city of the Shomronim (Samaria) enter not: But go rather to the lost sheep that have strayed from Beit Yisrael (house of Israel). And as you go, proclaim, saying, the

malchut ha Shamayim (the Kingdom of Heaven) is offered. Heal the sick, cleanse the lepers, raise the dead, and cast out shadim (devils): freely you have received, freely give. Take neither gold, nor silver, nor brass in your purses, Nor a bag for your journey, neither two coats, neither sandals, nor your staffs: for the workman is worthy of his food" Mattityahu (Matthew) 10:5-10.

"Then He said to His talmidim (disciples), the harvest truly is great, but the workers are few. Make tefillah (prayers) therefore to the Master of the harvest, that He will send forth workers into His harvest" Mattityahu (Matthew) 9:37-38.

Hara'chaman, hu yish'bor ulaynu may'al tzavaraynu V'hu yolikhaynu kom'miyut l'ar'tzaynu.

May the merciful One break the yoke of our oppression and lead us in dignity to our ancient homeland.

Hara'chaman, hu y'zakaynu limot hamasheeach, ul'chayay ha'olam haba. Amein.

May the merciful One enable us to live in the messianic age and in the world to come. Amein.

MIKRA-AZ YASHIR MOSHE

The Song of the Sea (also known as *Az Yashir Moshe* - the song of Moshe) is a chant of victory that was composed by Moshe to proclaim the greatness of YHWH. The song appears in the Book of Shemoth (Exodus), at Exodus 15:1-21. The additional verse 20 and 21 is the chorus of the song which was sung by Miriam and the other women. The Song of Moshe was first sung by Yisra'el after the miraclous crossing of the Red Sea, and it celebrates the destruction of the Mitzrayim (Egyptian) army during the crossing, and looks forward to their future conquest of Canaan. The chant is included in Jewish Siddurs, and recited daily in the morning shacharit services of the Synagogues.

MIKRA AZ YASHIR MOSHE

The proclamation of the song of Moshe

Face Yerushalem and recite this:

Barukh Atah, יהוה Eloheinu, Melekh haOlam, Asher kid'shanu b'mitzvotav v'tzivanu al Mitzvah mikra az yashir Moshe.

Praised are You, YHWH, our Elohim, King of the Universe, Who sanctified us with Mitzvot and has commanded us to proclaim the song of Moshe.

AZ YASHIR MOSHE

The song of Moshe

Face Yerushalem and chant this:

Shemoth (Exodus) 15:1-21

Siddur Bayit

1 *Az yashir Moshe u'venei Yisra'el et ha-shirah hazot la* יהוה, *vayomru lemor; a-shirah la-*יהוה *ki ga'oh ga'ah, sus v'rochevo ramah vayam.*
2 *Azi v'zimrat Yah, vayhi li-shu'ah; zeh eli v'aynvehu, elohei avi vaa-romen'nu.*
3 יהוה *ish milchah'mah;* יהוה *shemo.*
4 *Mar'kevot par'oh vecheilo yarah vaiyam; u'mivchar shali'shav tube'u v'yam-suf.*
5 *T'homot y'chasyumu; yardu vim'tzolot k'mo-aven.*
6 *Y'meenekha* יהוה, *nedari bako'ach; yeminekha* יהוה *tir'atz o'yev.*
7 *Uv'rov ge'onkha taharos kameikha; te'shalach charonekha, yokh'lemo kakash.*
8 *Uv'ruach apeikha ne'ermu mayim, ni'tzevu khmo-ned nozlim; kafe'u t'homot belev-yam.*
9 *Amar o'yev erdof asig a'chalek shalal; timla'emov nafshi, arik charbi, tori'sheimo yadi.*
10 *Nashaftah veruchakha kisamo yam; tzalalu ka'oferet, b'mayim adiyrim.*
11 *Mi-chamocha ba'elim* יהוה, *mi chamocha nedar bakodesh; nora tehilot oseh fele.*
12 *Nati'ta yemi'nekha, tivla'emo aretz.*
13 *Nachita v'chasdekha am-zu ga'aleta; nehalta v'azkha el-neveh kadeshekha.*
14 *Sham'u amim yirgazun; chil achaz, yoshevei pelasheet.*
15 *Az niv'halu alufei edom, eilei moav, yocha'zemo ra'ad; namogu kol yoshvei chena'an.*
16 *Tipol aleihem eimatah vafachad, bigdol z'roakha yidemu ka'aven; ad-ya'avor amekha* יהוה, *ad-ya'avor am-zu kanita.*
17 *Tevi'aemo vetit'aemo behar nacha'latikha, makhon leshiv'tikha pa'ayl'ta* יהוה *mikedash Adonei kon'nu yadeikha.*
18 יהוה *yimloch l'olam va'ed.*
19 *Kiva sus par'oh berikh'bo uv'farashav bayam, vayashev* יהוה *alehem et-mei hayam; uv'nei Yisra'el halechu vaya'bashah b'tokh hayam. f*
20 *Vatikhah Miriyam ha'niviah achot Aharon et-hatof b'yadah; vatei'tze'na chol-hanashim achareiha, b'tupim uvim'cholot.*
21 *Vataan lahem Miriyam; shiru lashem ki-ga'oh ga'ah, sus v'rokh'vo ramah vayam. s*

Shemoth (Exodus) 15:1-21

1 Then sang Moshe and the children of Yisrael this shir (song) to יהוה, and spoke, saying, I will sing to יהוה, for He has triumphed gloriously: the horse and his rider has He thrown into the sea.

2 YAH is my strength and shir, and He has become my Yahshua (salvation): He is my El, and I will hallel (praise) Him; my abba's Elohim, and I will exalt Him.

3 יהוה is a Man of war: יהוה is His Name.

4 Pharaoh's mirkavot (chariots) and his army has He cast into the sea: his chosen captains also are drowned in the Sea of Reeds.

5 The depths have covered them: they sank into the bottom as a stone.

6 Your Right Hand, O יהוה, has become tifereth (esteem) in power: Your Right Hand, O יהוה, has dashed in pieces the enemy.

7 And in the greatness of Your Excellency You have overthrown them that rose up against You: You sent forth Your anger, which consumed them as stubble.

8 And with the blast of Your nostrils the mayim were gathered together, the floods stood upright as a heap, and the depths became stiff in the lev (heart) of the sea.

9 The enemy said, I will pursue, I will overtake, I will divide the plunder; my desire shall be satisfied upon them; I will draw my sword, my hand shall destroy them.

10 You did blow with Your wind, the sea covered them: they sank as lead in the mighty mayim.

11 Me-chamocha (Who is like you), O יהוה, among the mighty ones? Who is like You, beautiful in set-apartness, awesome in tehillot (praises), doing wonders?

12 You stretched out Your Right Hand, the earth swallowed them.

13 You in Your rachamim (mercy) have led forth the people whom You have redeemed: You have guided them in Your strength to Your kadosh (set apart) dwelling.

14 The people shall hear, and be afraid: sorrow shall take hold on the inhabitants of Philistia.

15 Then the rulers of Edom shall be amazed; the mighty men of Moav, trembling shall take hold upon them; all the inhabitants of Kanaan shall melt away.

16 Fear and dread shall fall upon them; by the greatness of Your Arm they shall be as still as a stone; until Your people pass over, O יהוה, until the people pass over, whom You have purchased.
17 You shall bring them in, and plant them in the mountain of Your inheritance, in the place, O יהוה, which You have made for Yourself to dwell in, in the Kadosh-Place, O יהוה, that Your hands have established.
18 יהוה shall reign le-olam-va-ed.
19 For the horse of Pharaoh went in with his mirkavot and with his horsemen into the sea, and יהוה brought again the mayim (waters) of the sea upon them; but the children of Yisrael went on dry land in the midst of the sea.
20 And Miryam the neviyah (prophetess), the sister of Aharon, took a timbrel in her hand; and all the women went out after her with timbrels and with dances.
21 And Miryam answered them, Sing to יהוה, for He has triumphed gloriously; the horse and his rider has He thrown into the sea.

AZ YASHIR MOSIACH

The song of the Messsiah

The song of the Messiah along with the chant of the Moshe is identified in the Brit Chadashah as the song of the 144,000 elect who will serve YHWH as witnesses at the end of days. It is added here as an extension and reinforcement of the song of Moshe.

Face Yerushalem and chant this:

Gilyahna (Revelation) 15:3-4

3 *Vayashiru et-shirah Moshe ebed יהוה Elohim veshirat haseh leimor gedolim maa'seikha v'nif'layim יהוה Elohim Tseba'ot tzedek ve'emet d'rakekha Melek ha'goyim.*
4 *Milo yira'ahkha יהוה velo yiten kavod lo'shimkha ki-kadosh Atah l'vadekha ki kol-hagoyim yavo'u veyish tacha'vu lefanekha ki-niglu mish'petei tzedekha.*

Gilyahna (Revelation) 15:3-4

3 And they sing the shir of Moshe the eved of the Master יהוה, and the shir of the Lamb, saying, Great and marvelous are Your deeds, Master יהוה El-Shaddai; tzadik (righteous) and emet (true) are Your halachot (ways), O Melech of the Yisraelite kidushim (family).
4 Who shall not fear You, O Master יהוה, and glorify Your Name? For You alone are kadosh (set apart): for all nations shall come and worship before You; for Your mishpatim (judgements) are made manifest.

AMIDAH

The Amidah is the central prayer of Hebrew liturgy and is also the oldest dating back to time Ezra and the great Assembly. The Word *Amidah* literally means standing because it is recited while standing. It is also known as *Shemoneh Esrei* meaning eighteen because it originally consisted of eighteen blessings. An extra prayer was added after 100 AD against heretics, which is omitted here.

In Judaism it is customary to pray the Amidah three times a day. However, because of its length it is more appropriate to pray it at the end of the Shabbat to begin the new week. At the start of the Prayer it is customary to take three steps forward and at the end three steps back as was the custom of the Patriarchs.

TALLIT

The prayer shawl

While holding the Tallit in your hand say:

Barukh Atah יהוה, *Eloheinu Melech haOlam, Asher kidshanu b'mitzvotav v'tzivanu lit' atayf batzitzit.*

Praised are You YHWH, our Elohim King of the Universe, Who sanctified us with Mitzvot, and commands us to wrap ourselves in tzitzit.

THE SHEMA

The declaration of Yisra'el

Face Yerushalem and say:

Shema Yisra'el יהוה *Eloheinu,* יהוה *Echad!*
(Softly) *Barukh sheim k'vod mal'khuto l'olam va'ed!*

Hear, O Yisra'el: YHWH is our Elohim, the Eternal YHWH alone! (Devarim (Deuteronomy) 6:4) Praised is YHWH's glorious majesty forever and ever!

KADDISH

The exaltation

Adonai, s'fatai tifach, ufee yageed, t'hilatekah.

Sovereign Elohim open my lips, that my mouth may declare Your praise.

Yitgadal v'yitkadash sh'meih rab, Amein.
B'alma di-v'ra khir'utayh, v'yamleekh mal'khutayh b'cha-yaykhon uv'yomaykhon uv'cha-yay d'khol bayit Yisra'el, ba'agala uviz' man kareev, vim'ru Amein.
Y'hay sh'meih raba m'vorach l'olam ul'al'may al'ma-ya.
Yitbarakh v'yishtabach v'yitpa'ar v'yitronmam v'yitnasay v'yithadar v'yit'aleh v'yithalal sh'meih d'kud'sha, b'reekh hu, L'ayla min kol bir'khata v'sheerata tush'b'chata v'nechemata da'ameern b'alma v'imru. Amein.

Let the esteem of Elohim be extolled, Amein.
Let Elohim's great name be exalted in the world Whose creation Elohim willed. May Elohim rule in our own day, in our own lives, and in the life of all Yisra'el, and let us say Amein.
Lets Elohim's great name be praise forever and ever. Beyond all praises, songs and adorations that we can utter is the Set Apart One, the Blessed One, Whom we upraise, honour and exalt. And let us say Amein.

Barukh יהוה ham vorakh l'olam va'ed!

Praised be YHWH to Whom our praise is due, now and forever!

Siddur Bayit

1. AVOT V'IMHOT

The Elohim of our fathers

It is customary to bend the knees and bow while standing at both the start and end of the first blessing when saying *"Barukh Atah יהוה"* literally "Praise be YHWH."

Barukh Atah יהוה, Eloheinu vaylohay avoteinu V'imoteinu.
Elohay Avraham, Elohay Yitzchak, Vayloay Ya'akov. Elohay Sarah, Elohay Rivkah, Elohay Lay'ah Vaylohay Rachel.
Ha'El haGodol, haGibor v'haNora El Elyon.
Gomayl chasadim tovim, v'konay hakol, v'zochayr chas'day avot v'imahot, umayvee g'ulah liv'nay v'nayhem, l'ma'an sh'mo b'ahavah. Melech ozayr umosheea umagayn.
Barukh Atah יהוה, magayn Avraham v'ezrat Sarah.

Praised be our YHWH, the Sovereign of our fathers and our mothers: The Elohim of Avraham, Elohim of Yitzchak, and Elohim of Ya'akov; Elohim of Sarah, Elohim of Rivkah, Elohim of Lay'ah and Elohim of Rachel;
Great, mighty and awesome Elohim, Elohim supreme. Rulers of all the living, Your ways are ways of love.
You remember the faithfulness of our ancestor, and in love bring redemption to their children's children for the sake of Your name. You are Sovereign and our Help, our Redeemer and Shield.
Praised are You YHWH, Shield of Avraham, Protector of Sarah.

2. G'VUROT

The Elohim Who remembers

Atah gobor l'olam יהוה, m'cha-yay maytim Atah, rav l'hosheea.
M'khakayl cha-yim b'chesaid, m'cha-yay maytim B'rachamim, rabeen.
Somaykh nof'lim, v'rofay cholim, umateer asurim, um'ka-yaym emunato lishanay afar.

Mee khamokha, ba'al g'vurot, umi domay lakh, Melech maymeet um'chayeh u'matzmeeach yeshuah: V'ne'eman Atah l'hacha-yot maytim.
Barukh Atah יהוה, M'cha-yay hamaytim.

Eternal is your might, O YHWH, Who resurrects the dead. Great is Your power to save! With love You sustain the living, with great compassion You resurrect the dead.

You send help to the falling and healing to the sick; You bring freedom to the captive and keep faith with those who sleep in the dust. Who is like You Mighty One? Who is like You, source of mercy: In compassion You sustain the life of your children. And You are faithful to restore the dead to life. We praise You YHWH, Who resurrects the dead.

3. KADUSAH

The Set Apart Elohim

It is customary to bend the knees and bow when saying "*Kadosh, Kadosh, Kadosh*" literally "Set Apart, Set Apart, Set Apart."

N'kadaysh et shim'kha ba'olam, k'shaym shemakdeeshim.
Oto bish'may marom, kakatuv al yad n'vee'ekha V'kara zay el-zay v'amar:
Kadosh, Kadosh, Kadosh יהוה Tz'va'ot, m'lo khol ha'aretz k'vodo!
Adeer Adeereinu, יהוה adoneinu, Mah adeer shim'kha b'khol ha'aretz!
Barukh k'vod יהוה mim'komo. Echad hu Eloheinu, hu Aveinu, Hu Malkeinu, hu Moshee'aynu; V'hu yashmee'aynu b'rachamav l'aynay kol chai: "Ani יהוה Eloheikhem!" Yimlokh יהוה l'olam, Eloha-yikh Tziyon, L'dor vador. Halleluyah!
L'dor vador nageed godlekha, ul'naytzach n'tzachim k'dushat'kha nakdeesh. V'shivchakha, Eloheinu, mipeenu lo yamush l'olam va'ed.
Barukh Atah יהוה, ha'El haKadosh.

We sanctify Your name on Earth, even as all things, to the ends of time and space, proclaim Your Set Apartness; and in the words of the prophet we say;
Kadosh, Kadosh, Kadosh is YHWH of Hosts; the fullness of the whole Earth is Elohim's esteem! (Yeshayahu (Isaiah) 6:3).
How majestic is YHWH's presence in all the earth! Praised is the esteem of YHWH in Heaven and Earth. (Yechezkel (Ezekiel) 3:12).
YHWH alone is our Elohim and our Creator, YHWH is our Ruler and Helper and in Elohim's great mercy YHWH reveals Elohim in the sight of all the living: "I am YHWH your Elohim!"
YHWH shall reign for ever; your Elohim, O Zion from generation to generation. Halleluyah! (Tehillim (Psalms) 146:10.
To all generations we will make known Your greatness, and to all eternity proclaim Your Set Apartness. Your praise O Elohim, shall never depart from our lips.
Praised is YHWH, the Set Apart Elohim.

4. BINAH

Source of wisdom

Atah chonayn l'adam da'at um'lamayd le'enosh binah.
Chonaynu meit'cha day'ah uvinah v'haskayl.
Barukh Atah יהוה, chonayn hada'at.

By Your grace we have the power to gain knowledge and to learn wisdom.
Favour us with the knowledge, wisdom and insight, that comes from You.
We praise You O YHWH, gracious giver of Knowledge.

5. TESHUVAH

Source of repentance

Hashivaynu avinu l'toratekha v'karbaynu malkaynu l'avodatekha,
v'hachziraynu bit'shuva shlayma l'fenekha.
Barukh Atah יהוה, Harotzeh bitshuvah.

Help us, our Abba, to return to Your instruction; draw us, our King to Your service; and cause us to return to You in perfect repentance.
We praise You O YHWH, Who delights in repentance.

6. SHILICHAH

Source of forgiveness

S'lach lanu avinu ki chatanu, m'chol lanu Mal'keinu ki fasha'nu, ki El tov v'salach Atah.
Barukh Atah יהוה, Chanun hamarbeh lisloach.

Forgive us, our Abba, for we have sinned; pardon us, our King, for we have transgressed;
For you are eager to pardon and forgive.
We praise You O YHWH, Who is merciful and always ready to forgive.

7. G'ULAH

Source of redemption

R'ayh na von'aynu, v'reevah reevaynu, umaheir lag'aoleinu gu'lah shlaymah l'ma'an shmekha. Ki El golayl chazak Atah.
Barukh Atah יהוה, Goayl Yisra'el.

Look upon our affliction and help us in our need; O mighty redeemer and redeem us speedily for Your name's sake. Praised are you O YHWH, redeemer of Yisra'el.

8. R'FUAH

Source of health

Rfa'aynu יהוה v'nayrafay, hosheaynu v'nivashay'ah, ki thilateinu Atah v'ha'alayh arukhah umarpay l'khol makoteinu ki El rofay rachaman vne'eman Atah.
Barukh Atah יהוה, Rofayh cholay amo Yisra'el.

Heal us, YHWH, and we will be healed; Save us and we will be saved. Grant us a perfect healing to all our infirmities, for You, almighty King, are a faithful and merciful healer. Praised are you YHWH, the healer of the sick of His people Yisra'el.

9. BIRKAT HASHANIM

Source of wealth

Baraykh aleinu, יהוה Eloheinu, et-hashanah Hazot v'et-kol-minay t'vuatah l'tovah.
V'ten b'rakha al p'nay ha'adamah vsab'aynu mituvekha, uvaraykh shanateinu kashanim hatovot.
Barukh Atah יהוה, M'varaykh hashanim.

Bless this year for us, O YHWH our Elohim, together with all the varieties of its produce, for our welfare.
Bestow Your blessing on the Earth that all Your children may share its abundance in peace. O satisfy us with Your goodness, and bless our year like the best of years.
Praised are You YHWH, for You bless Earth's seasons from year to year.

10. CHEIRUT

Source of restoration

T'kah b'shofar gadol l'chayruteinu, v'sa nays l'kabaytz galuyoteinu v'kabtzaynu m'hayrah yachad may'arba kan'fot ha'aretz lar'tzaynu.
Barukh Atah יהוה, M'kabaytz nid'chay amo Yisra'el.

Sound the great shofar to proclaim our freedom, raise high the banner of liberation to gather our exiles and gather us from the four corners of the Earth.
Praised are You YHWH, Who gathers the dispersed of Your people Yisra'el.

11. MISHPAT

Source of justice

Al shof'tay eretz sh'fukh ruchekha, v'hadreekhaym b'mish'p'tay tzidikekha, um'lokh aleinu Atah l'vadekha, b'chesaid uv'rachamim.
Barukh Atah יהוה, Melech ohayv tz'dakah umisphat.

Bestow your Spirit upon the rulers of all lands; guide them that they may govern justly.
Then shall love and compassion be enthroned among us.
Praised are You, YHWH, our King Who loves righteousness and justice.

12. AI HATZADIKIM

Source of righteousness

Al ha'tzadikim v'al ha'chasedim v'al gayray hatzedek v'aleinu ye'hemu rach'maykha, יהוה Eloheinu, v'tayn sakhar tov l'khol habot'chim b'shimkha be'emet, v'sim chel'keinu imahem l'olam.
Barukh Atah יהוה, Mish'an umiv'tach la'tzadikim.

For the righteous and faithful of all humankind, for all who join themselves to our people, for all who put their trust YHWH our Elohim and for all honest men and women, we ask Your favour. Grant that we may be always numbered among them.
Praised are You YHWH, Staff and Support of the righteous.

13. YERUSHALEM

Restorer of Yerushalem

Sh'khon יהוה Eloheinu b'tokh Yerushalem irekha v'yhi shalom bish'arayha, v'shal'va b'layv yosh'vayha, v'torat'kah mitzi'on tetzeh udvarkha mirushalem.
Barukh Atah יהוה, Boneh Yerushalem.

Let YHWH our Elohim presence be manifest in Yerushalem Your city. Establish peace in her gates and quietness in the hearts of all who dwell there. Let Your Torah go forth from Zion, Your Word from Yerushalem.
Praised are you YHWH, builder of Yerushalem.

14. YESHUA

Saviour of the World

Et tzemach tzedakah m'hayrah ta'tzmecha v'keren yeshua tarum kin'umeecha ki lishu'atekha kiveinu kol hayom.
Barukh Atah יהוה, Matzmeeach keren yeshua.

Speedily let the branch of righteousness blossom and flourish and let the light of deliverance shine forth according to Your Word, for we await all day Your salvation.
Praised are You YHWH, Who causes the light of salvation to dawn for all the world.

15. SHEMA KOLAYNU

Who answers prayer

Shema koleinu יהוה Eloheinu chus v'rachaym aleinu, ut'kabayl b'rachamayn uvratzon et t'filateinu, ki El shomay'a t'filot v'ta'chanunim Atah.
Barukh Atah יהוה, Shomayh tifilah.

Hear our voice, YHWH our Elohim; have compassion upon us and accept our prayer in mercy and with favour, for You are a Elohim Who hears prayer and supplication.
Praised are You YHWH, Who hearken to prayer.

16. AVODAH

Who favours His people

*R'tzay, יהוה Eloheinu, b'am'kha Yisra'el ut'filatam b'ahavah t'kabayl, ut'hi l'ratzon tamed avodat Yisra'el amekha.
Barukh Atah יהוה, She'ot'kha l'vad'kha b'yir'ah na'avod.*

Be favourable YHWH our Elohim, toward Your people Yisra'el and receive their prayers with love. May the worship of Your people Yisra'el always be acceptable to You.
Praised are You YHWH, Whom alone we serve.

17. HODA'AH

Thanksgiving for His unfailing mercies

*Modim anachnu lakh, sha'atah hu יהוה Eloheinu vaylohay avoteinu v'imateinu l'olam va'ed. Tzur cha-yaynu, magayn yish'aynu, Atah hu l'dor vador. Nodeh l'kha un'sapayr t'hilatekha, al-cha-yaynu ham'surim v'yadekha, v'al-nishmoteinu hap'kudot lakh, v'al nisekha sheb'khol-yom imanu, v'al-nifl'otekha v'tovotekha sheb'khol-ayt, erev vavoker v'tzohora-yim. Hatov ki lo-khalu rachamekha v'ham'rachaym ki-lo tamu chasadekha, may'olam kiveenu lakh.
V'al kulam yitbarach v'yitromam shim'kha, Malkeinu, tamed l'olam va'ed. V'khol hacha-yim yodukha (selah), veehal'luet shim'kha be'emet, ha'El yeshu ateinu v'ezrateinu (selah):
Barukh Atah יהוה, Hatov shim'kha ul'kha na'ay l'hodot.*

We give thanks to You that You are YHWH our Elohim and the Elohim of our fathers forever and ever. Through every generation you have been the rock of our lives, the shield of our salvation. We are thankful to You and give You praise for our lives that are committed into Your hands, for our souls that are under your direction and for Your miracles that are with us daily, and for Your wonders and Your act of goodness that are with us at all times, evening, morning and noon. O Beneficent One, your mercies never fail; We have hoped for Your eternally.

For all these acts may Your name be praised and exalted O King, always and forever. Let every living thing give thanks to You (a short pause) and praise Your name in truth, O Elohim, our salvation and our help (a short pause.)
Praised are You YHWH, Whose Name is the Beneficent One, and to Whom it is fitting to give thanks.

18. SIM SHALOM

For peace

Sim shalom, tovah uv'rakhah, chen, vachesaid, v'rachameen, aleinu v'al kol Yisra'el amekah. Amein.

Peace, happiness, and blessing, favour and love and mercy, may these descend on us, on all Yisra'el and all the world. Amein.

SHABBAT AMIDAH

The Shabbat Amidah is a composition of several prayers from the Amidah and Brit Chadashah that are said during the day in one's home before sunset.

AVOT V'IMAHOT

Avinu ani, s'fatai tiftach, ufee yageed t'hilatekah.

My Father, open my lips, that my mouth may declare Your praise.

Barukh Atah יהוה, Eloheinu vaylohay avoteinu V'imoteinu.
Elohay Avraham, Elohay Yitzchak, Vayloay Ya'akov. Elohay Sarah, Elohay Rivkah, Elohay Lay'ah Vaylohay Rachel.
Ha'El haGodol, haGibor v'haNora El Elyon.
Gomayl chasadim tovim, v'konay hakol, v'zochayr chas'day avot v'imahot, umayvee g'ulah liv'nay v'nayhem, l'ma'an sh'mo b'ahavah. Melech ozayr umosheea umagayn.
Barukh Atah יהוה, magayn Avraham v'ezrat Sarah.

Praised be our YHWH, the Sovereign of our fathers and our mothers: The Elohim of Avraham, Elohim of Yitzchak, and Elohim of Ya'akov; Elohim of Sarah, Elohim of Rivkah, Elohim of Lay'ah and Elohim of Rachel;
Great, mighty and awesome Elohim, Elohim supreme. Rulers of all the living, Your ways are ways of love.
You remember the faithfulness of our ancestor, and in love bring redemption to their children's children for the sake of Your name.
You are Sovereign and our Help, our Redeemer and Shield.
Praised are You YHWH, Shield of Avraham, Protector of Sarah.

G'VUROT

Atah gobor l'olam יהוה, m'cha-yay maytim Atah, rav l'hosheea.
M'khakayl cha-yim b'chesaid, m'cha-yay maytim B'rachamim, rabeen.

Somaykh nof'lim, v'rofay cholim, umateer asurim, um'ka-yaym emunato lishanay afar.
Mee khamokha, ba'al g'vurot, umi domay lakh, Melech maymeet um'chayeh u'matzmeeach yeshuah: V'ne'eman Atah l'hacha-yot maytim.
Barukh Atah יהוה, M'cha-yay hamaytim.

Eternal is your might, O YHWH, Who resurrects the dead. Great is Your power to save! With love You sustain the living, with great compassion You resurrect the dead.

You send help to the falling and healing to the sick; You bring freedom to the captive and keep faith with those who sleep in the dust. Who is like You Mighty One? Who is like You, source of mercy: In compassion You sustain the life of your children. And You are faithful to restore the dead to life. We praise You YHWH, Who resurrects the dead.

KADUSAH

N'kadaysh et shim'kha ba'olam, k'shaym shemakdeeshim.
Oto bish'may marom, kakatuv al yad n'vee'ekha V'kara zay elzay v'amar:
Kadosh, Kadosh, Kadosh יהוה Tz'va'ot, m'lo khol ha'aretz k'vodo!
Adeer Adeereinu, יהוה adoneinu, Mah adeer shim'kha b'khol ha'aretz!
Barukh k'vod יהוה mim'komo. Echad hu Eloheinu, hu Aveinu, Hu Malkeinu, hu Moshee'aynu; V'hu yashmee'aynu b'rachamav l'aynay kol chai: "Ani יהוה Eloheikhem!" Yimlokh יהוה l'olam, Eloha-yikh Tziyon, L'dor vador. Halleluyah!
L'dor vador nageed godlekha, ul'naytzach n'tzachim k'dushat'kha nakdeesh. V'shivchakha, Eloheinu, mipeenu lo yamush l'olam va'ed.
Barukh Atah יהוה, ha'El haKadosh.

We sanctify Your name on Earth, even as all things, to the ends of time and space, proclaim Your Set Apartness; and in the words of the prophet we say;

Kadosh, Kadosh, Kadosh is YHWH of Hosts; the fullness of the whole Earth is Elohim's esteem! (Yeshayahu (Isaiah) 6:3).

How majestic is YHWH's presence in all the earth! Praised is the esteem of YHWH in Heaven and Earth. (Yechezkel (Ezekiel) 3:12).

YHWH alone is our Elohim and our Creator, YHWH is our Ruler and Helper and in Elohim's great mercy YHWH reveals Elohim in the sight of all the living: "I am YHWH your Elohim!"

YHWH shall reign for ever; your Elohim, O Zion from generation to generation. Halleluyah! (Tehillim (Psalms) 146:10.

To all generations we will make known Your greatness, and to all eternity proclaim Your Set Apartness. Your praise O Elohim, shall never depart from our lips.

Praised is YHWH, the Set Apart Elohim.

TEFILLAT HA-TALMIDIM

Aveinu Shebashamayim yitkadash Sh'mekah.
Tavo mal'khutekha yay'asay ratzon'kha k'mo bashamayim kayn ba'aretz.
Et-lechem chukaynu ten-lanu hayom.
Us'lach-lanu et-chovotaynu ka'asher salachnu gam-anachnu lacha-yavanu.
Va'al tavee'aynu leeday nisayon ki im-chal'tzaynu min-hara ki l'kah hamamlakha v'hagavura v'hatif'eret l'ol'may olameen. Amein.

Our Abba Who is in the shamayim, kadosh shmecha.

Your malchut come. Your ratzon be done in the earth, as it is in the shamayim.

And lead us not into temptation, but deliver us from evil: For Yours is the malchut, and the power, and the tifereth, le-olam-va-ed. Amein.

Give us today our daily lechem.

And forgive us our debts, as we forgive our debtors.

V'SHAM'RU

V'sham'ru v'nay Yisra'el et haShabbat, la'asot et ha'Shabbat b'reet olam.
Baynay uvayn b'nay Yisra'el ot hay l'olam, ki shayshet yameem asah Adonai et ha'shamayim v'et ha'aretz, uvayom hash'vi'i shavat va-yinafash.

The people of Yisra'el shall keep the Shabbat observing the Shabbat in every egeneration as a covenant for all time.
It is a sign forever between Me and the people of Yisra'el, for six days the Eternal Elohim made the heaven and earth, taking rest and refreshment on the seventh day. (Shemoth (Exodus) 31:16-17).

AVODAH

R'tzay, יהוה Eloheinu, b'am'kha Yisra'el ut'filatam b'ahavah t'kabayl, ut'hi l'ratzon tamed avodat Yisra'el amekha.
Barukh Atah יהוה, She'ot'kha l'vad'kha b'yir'ah na'avod.

Be favourable YHWH our Elohim, toward Your people Yisra'el and receive their prayers with love. May the worship of Your people Yisra'el always be acceptable to You.
Praised are You YHWH, Whom alone we serve.

HODA'AH

Modim anachnu lakh, sha'atah hu יהוה Eloheinu vaylohay avoteinu v'imateinu l'olam va'ed. Tzur cha-yaynu, magayn yish'aynu, Atah hu l'dor vador. Nodeh l'kha un'sapayr t'hilatekha, al-cha-yaynu ham'surim v'yadekha, v'al-nishmoteinu hap'kudot lakh, v'al nisekha sheb'khol-yom imanu, v'al-nifl'otekha v'tovotekha sheb'khol-ayt, erev vavoker v'tzohora-yim. Hatov ki lo-khalu rachamekha v'ham'rachaym ki-lo tamu chasadekha, may'olam kiveenu lakh.
V'al kulam yitbarach v'yitromam shim'kha, Malkeinu, tamed l'olam va'ed. V'khol hacha-yim yodukha (selah), veehal'luet shim'kha be'emet, ha'El yeshu ateinu v'ezrateinu (selah):

Barukh Atah יהוה, Hatov shim'kha ul'kha na'ay l'hodot.

We give thanks to You that You are YHWH our Elohim and the Elohim of our fathers forever and ever. Through every generation you have been the rock of our lives, the shield of our salvation. We are thankful to You and give You praise for our lives that are committed into Your hands, for our souls that are under your direction and for Your miracles that are with us daily, and for Your wonders and Your act of goodness that are with us at all times, evening, morning and noon. O Beneficent One, your mercies never fail; We have hoped for Your eternally.

SIM SHALOM

Sim shalom, tovah uv'rakhah, chen, vachesaid, v'rachameen, aleinu v'al kol Yisra'el amekah. Amein.

Peace, happiness, and blessing, favour and love and mercy, may these descend on us, on all Yisra'el and all the world. Amein.

EIN KELOHEINU

Ein Keloheinu "there is none like our Elohim" is a well known Jewish hymn. The prayer is said during Shabbat and festival services, although in some traditions it is said daily often quietly by every person for themselves. The background for the prayer is that its 20 sentences each count as a blessing. Rabbinal teachings exhort keepers of the Torah to make at least 100 blessings daily. *Ein Keloheinu* was designed to ensure that everybody would say at least 100 blessings a day. The goal is to enrich our vocabulary with words of blessings.

EIN KELOHEINU

There is none like our Elohim

*Ein keloheinu, en kadoneinu, en kemalkeinu, en kemoshienu,
mi keloheinu, mi kadoneinu, mi kemalkeinu, mi kemoshienu,
nodeh leloheinu, nodeh ladoneinu, nodeh lemalkeinu, nodeh lemoshienu,
barukh Eloheinu, barukh Adoneinu, barukh Malkeinu, Barukh Moshienu.
Atah hu Eloheinu, Atah hu Adoneinu, Atah hu Malkeinu, Atah hu Mosheinu.
Atah hu shehiqtiru aboteinu, lefanekha eth qetoreth hasamim.*

There is none like our Elohim, There is none like our Master,
There is none like our King, there is none like our Saviour.
Who is like our Elohim? Who is like our Master? Who is like our King? Who is like our Saviour?
Let us thank our Elohim, let us thank our Master, let us thank our King, let us thank our Saviour.
Praised be our Elohim, praised be our Master, praised be our King, praised be our Saviour.
You are our Elohim, You are our Master, You are our King, You are our Saviour.
You are the one before whom our fathers offered the spice offering.

ASHREI

Tehillim (Psalm) 145 is the only Psalm to bear the title *tehillah* (literally "praise") from which the entire book of Psalms takes its Hebrew name, *Tehillim*. It is alphabetic with the strophe of the letter *nun* missing. A Talmudic homily suggests that this is because the letter *nun* also begins a verse prophesying the destruction of Yisra'el (Ahmos (Amos) 5:2; Ber. 4b). According to Kabbalah, Psalms are not recited during night time hours therefore it is usually recited during the morning and afternoon prayer. However, because of its length it is more appropriate to pray it at the end of the Shabbat to begin the new week.

TEHILLAH L'DAVID

The Praise of David

Barukh Atah יהוה, *Eloheinu Melech haOlam, Asher kid'shanu b'mitzvotav v'tzivanu likro et haHalel.*

Praised are You YHWH, our Elohim King of the Universe, Who has sanctified us us with His commandments and commanded us to praise Him with the Psalms.

Tehillim (Psalm 145)

Aromime'kha, Elohay ha'Melech; va'avarcha shimcha l'olam va'ed.
B'chol-yom avarchecha, va'al'lecha shim'kha l'olam va'ed.

I will extol You, my Elohim, O Melech; and I will bless Your name le-olam-va-ed.
Every day will I bless You; and I will hallel Your name le-olam-va-ed.

Gadol יהוה *umhulal me'od, v'ligdulato ein cheker.*
Dor l'dor y'shabach ma'asekha, ugvurotekha yagidu.

Great is YHWH, and greatly to be praised; and His greatness is unsearchable.
One generation shall hallel Your works to another, and shall declare Your mighty acts.

Hadar k'vod hode'kha, v'divrei nifli'otekha asicha.

I will speak of the beautiful honor of Your majesty, and of Your wonderful works.

V'ezuz nor'otekha yomeru, Ugdulate'kha asp'reina.
Zecher rav-tuvekha yabi'u, V'tzidikat'kha y'ranaynu.

And men shall speak of the might of Your awesome acts: and I will declare Your greatness.
They shall abundantly utter the memory of Your great tov, and shall shir about Your tzedakah.

Chanun v'rachum יהוה, erech apayim ugdal chesaid.
Tov יהוה l'kol, v'rachamav al-kol-ma'asav.

YHWH is full of favor, and full of rachamim; slow to anger, and of great rachamim.
YHWH is tov to all: and His tender rachamim are over all His works.

Y'hiyu l'ratzon im'rei fi v'hegyon libi l'fanekha, יהוה tzuri v'goali. Amein.

May the words of my mouth and the meditations of my heart be acceptable to You, YHWH, my Rock and my Redeemer. Amein.
(Tehillim (Psalm) 19:15)

AVINU MALKEINU

This is the traditional version of this prayer is recited or sung during during Rosh Hashanah, Yom Kippur, on the Ten Days Awe (Repentance). In the Ashkenazic tradition, it is recited on all fast days; in the Sephardic tradition only because it is recited for the Ten Days of Repentance does it occur on the fast days of Yom Kippur and the Fast of Gedaliah. The origin of this prayer is not certain althought the Talmud (T.B. Ta'anith 25b) records Rabbi Akiba (died 135 C.E) reciting two verses each beginning "Our Father, Our King" in a prayer to end a drought successfully.

Throughout the Ten Days of Repentance, five lines of Avinu Malkeinu that refer to book of life include the word *"kotveinu"* - Inscribe us. During Ne'ila - the final prayers of Yom Kippur, this is replaced with *"chotmeinu"* - seal us. This reflects the Jewish belief that on Rosh Hashanah all is written and revealed and on Yom Kippur all decrees for the coming year are sealed. When recited on a fast day the phrase *"barech aleinu"* - bless us is recited instead of the usual *"chadesh aleinu"*.

AVINU MALKEINU

Our Father, our King

Avinu Malkeinu sh'ma kolenu,
Avinu Malkeinu chatanu l'faneicha,
Avinu Malkeinu chamol aleinu,
Ve'al olaleinu vetapeinu,

Avinu Malkeinu,
Kaleh dever,
vecherev vera'av mealeinu,
Avinu Malkeinu,
kaleh chol tsar,
Umastin mealeinu,

Avinu Malkeinu,
Avinu Malkeinu,
Kat'veinu besefer chayim tovim,
Avinu Malkeinu chadesh aleinu,
Chadesh aleinu shanah tovah,

Sh'ma kolenu,
Sh'ma kolenu,
Sh'ma kolenu,

Avinu Malkeinu,
Avinu Malkeinu,
Chadesh aleinu shanah tovah,

Avinu Malkeinu,
Sh'ma kolenu. (x4)

Our Father our King, hear our voice,
Our Father our King, we have sinned before you,
Our Father our King, have compassion upon us,
and upon our children,

Our Father our King,
Bring an end to pestilence,
war, and famine around us,
Our Father our King,
Bring an end to all trouble,
and oppression around us,

Our Father our King,
Our Father our King,
Inscribe us in the book of (good) life,
Our father our King, renew upon us,
Renew upon us a good year,

Hear our voice,
Hear our voice,
Hear our voice,

Our Father our King,
Our Father our King,
Renew upon us a good year,

Our Father our King,
Hear our voice. (x4)

KADDISH

The Mourner's *Kaddish* is an ancient prayer of praise written in Aramaic that expresses a longing for the establishment of YHWH's Kingdom on Earth. Originally it was recited by rabbis' when they had finished giving their sermons (Kaddish D'Rabanan - the *Rabbi's Kaddish*) in time the prayer was modified and became associated with mourning (*Kaddish Yatom*) and Yom Kippur (*Kaddish Shalem*). The Mourner's Kaddish is infact not a prayer about death but about life. The words of the Kaddish provide lasting comfort by stressing the greatness and sovereignty of Elohim even in the most harrowing of life circumstances. The word *kaddish* means sanctification, referring to the setting apart of YHWH's Name *(Kiddush haShem)*. Jewish tradition requires that Kaddish be recited during the first eleven months following the death of a loved one and thereafter on each anniversary of the death (called the *Yahrtzeit)*. This is called *Avelut*. As seen already their are several versions of the Kiddish for different purposes and times of the year. This version is the Shephardic based and is oldest of the traditions.

Note: It is custom to bow on the words *"Oseh shalom bimrova"* in all directions, East, West, North and South, to acknowledge the presence of Elohim everywhere. The cues have been inserted into the text.

Yitgadal v'yit'kadash sh'mei rabah.
B'alma div'ra khir'utayn, v'yamleekh mal'khutayn,
V'yatzmach purkanein, vikarayv m'sheechein. Amein.
B'cha-yeikhon uv'yomeikhon uv'cha-yei d'chol beit Yisra'el,
ba'agalah uviz'man kariv, v'im'ru. Amein, Amein.
Y'hei sh'mei rabah m'vorakh l'alam ul'al'mei al'ma-ya.
Yit'barakh v'yish'tabakh v'yit'pa'ar v'yit'romam v'yit'nasei
v'yit'hadar v'yit'alei v'yit'halal sh'meih d'kudsha, b'rekh Hu,
l'ayla min kol bir'khata v'sherata tush'b'chata v'nechemata
da'ameran b'alma v'imru. Amein, Amein.
Al Yisra'el v'al rabanan v'al talmedayhon v'al kol-talmeday
talmedayhon, d'as'keen b'ora-yi'ta kadish'ta,

de ve'at'ra hadein v'de v'khol-atar va'atar, y'hay lana ul'hon ul'khon china v'chisda v'rachamei, min kodam maray sh'maya v'ar'a v'imru. Amein Amein.
Y'hei sh'lama raba min sh'maya v'chayim v'sava vishu'ah v'nechemah v'shayzava ur'fuah ug'ulah
usleechah v'khaparah v'rayvach v'hatzalah lanu ul'khol-amo Yisra'el v'imru. Amein, Amein.
(Now bow take three steps back and bow to the left)
Oseh shalom bim'romav, (bow to right) *Hu ya'aseh shalom aleinu* (bow forward) *v'al kol Yisra'el v'imru. Amein.*
(Remain in this place for a few moments then take three steps forward).

Let the esteem of Elohim be extolled, let Elohim's great name be magnified and sactified in the world whose creation He willed.
May His Kingdom come and may His salvation prosper and may His Anointed One draw near. Amein.
May it be during our lives, even in our days and in the lives of all the house of Yisra'el, swifly and soon and let us say Amein, Amein.
Let Elohim's esteemed name be praised for ever and ever. May His great name be blessed, praised, magnified, exalted, extolled, mighty, upraised and lauded. Praised be He and let us say. Amein.
Beyond all praises, songs, adorations and consolation, that are uttered in the Universe, and let us say Amein, Amein.
Upon Yisra'el and upon the teachers and upon their students and upon their disciples, who study the sacred Scriptures, who are in our land and among other lands. May the favour, goodness and mercy of the Eternal One of heaven and earth be upon them and us and let us say, Amein, Amein.
May their be peace from above, life, wellbeing, salvation, consolation, comfort, healing, redemption, forgiveness, atonement, deliverance and the promise of life to come for us and for all Your people Yisra'el and let us say Amein, Amein.
(Now bow take three steps back and bow to the left) **May the One who causes shalom to reign in the Universe,** (bow to right) **grant us shalom** (bow forward) **and upon all Yisra'el** (bow to the left) **and let us say. Amein.**

(Remain in this place for a few moments then take three steps forward).

Zichronam livracha.

May their memories be for blessing.

KADOSH

This is an early version of prayer that was used in Orthodox liturgies. It is a custom to rise up on one's toes when we say the *Kadosh Kadosh Kadosh* which harmonizes us with the reaction of Malakim (Angels) when they worship in Heaven.

Kadosh, Kadosh, Kadosh
יהוה *Tz'va'ot m'lo khol ha'aretz k'vodo*

Exalted, Exalted, Exalted YHWH of Hosts; all the Earth is full of His esteem.

HAL'LUYAH

Va'anachnu n'varei'kh ya mei'atah v'ad olam hal'luyah.

We shall bless You now and forever, Halleluyah!
(Tehillim (Psalm) 115:18)

KOL HANESHAMAH

Kol han'shama t'halei Ya, hal'luyah!

Let every soul praise Yah. Halleluyah!
(Tehillim (Psalm) 150.

BIRKHOT AHARONIC

The Kohen or Priestly blessing is one of the oldest of Scriptural prayers and was part of the Temple service (Bamidbar (Numbers) 6:24-26). The Aharonic Priesthood performed this blessing until the destruction of the Temple in 70 C.E. Under Rabbinic tradition if a non Kohen (non Priest) is present then the father or the leader of the ceremony should say it.

BIRKHOT AHARONIC

The Aharonic priestly blessing

Yevarekh'kha יהוה *v'yishme'rekha.*
Yah-er יהוה *panav elekha v'yechunekha.*
Yisaah יהוה *panav elechah v'yasem lekhah shalom.*

"יהוה *bless you, and keep you.*
יהוה *make His face shine upon you, and be gracious to you.*
יהוה *lift up His countenance upon you, and give you shalom."*

HA-TORAH

Ha-Torah literally means "the Torah" and is the weekly portion of the Torah that is read on the Shabbat. This is what is said before reading the Torah and after reading Torah on the Shabbat. It can also be said at any time you read the Torah.

HA-TORAH

The blessing before the reading of the Torah

Bar'khu et יהוה Ham'vorach!
Barukh יהוה Ham'vorach l'olam va'ed!
Barukh Atah יהוה, Eloheinu Melech haOlam, Asher bachar-banu mikol-ha'amim v'natan lanu et-torato. Barukh Atah יהוה, Notein haTorah.

Praise YHWH to Whom our praise is due!
Praised be YHWH, to Whom our praise is due, now and forever!
Praised be YHWH, our Elohim King of the Universe, who has chosen us from all peoples by giving us the Torah.
We praise You YHWH, Giver of the Torah.

The blessing after the reading of the Torah

Barukh Atah יהוה, Eloheinu melech haOlam, Asher natan lanu Torat emet v'chayei olam nata b'tocheinu.
Barukh Atah יהוה, Notein haTorah.

Praised are you YHWH, our Elohim King of the Universe, Who has given us a Torah of truth, implanting within us eternal life.
We praise You YHWH, Giver of the Torah.

HAFTORAH

This is what is said before reading the Haftarah and after reading the Haftarah on the Shabbat. Haftarah literally means "conclusion." The Haftarah is the weekly portion from the books of the Neviim or Prophets that is read as part of the Shabbat Torah reading. It can also be said at any time you read the Neviim.

HAFTORAH

The blessing before the reading of the Prophets

Barukh Atah יהוה, Eloheinu Melech haOlam, Asher bachar b'nivi'im tovim, v'ratzah v'div'rayhem hane'emarim be'emet.
Barukh Atah יהוה, habochayr batorah, uv'Moshay avdo, uv'Yisra'el amo uv'nivee'ay ha'emet vatzedek.

Praised are You YHWH, our Elohim King of the Universe, Who has called faithful prophets to speak words of truth.
Praised be YHWH, for the revelation of the Torah, for Moses Your servant and Yisra'el Your people, and for the prophets of truth and righteousness.

The blessing after the reading of the Prophets

Barukh Atah יהוה, Eloheinu melech haOlam, Tzur kol-ha'Olamim, tzadik b'khol-hadorot, ha'El hane'eman, ha'omayr v'osay, ham'dabayr um'ka-yaym, shekol d'varav, emet vatzedek.
Al ha'Torah, v'al ha'avoda, v'al han'vee'im V'al yom ha'Shabbat ha'zay, shenatata-lanu, יהוה Eloheinu, lik'dushah v'lim'nucha, l'Khavod ul'tif'aret, al-hakol, יהוה Eloheinu, anachnu modim lakh, um'var'khim otakh.
Yitbarakh shim'kha b'fee kol chai tameed l'olam va'ed.
Barukh Atah יהוה, M'kadaysh ha'Shabbat.

Praised are you YHWH, our Elohim King of the Universe, the Rock of all creation, the Righteous One of all generations, the faithful Elohim Whose word is deed, Whose every command is just and true.

For the Torah, for the privilege of worship, for the prophets, and for this Shabbat that You, our Eternal Elohim, have given us for set apartness and rest, for honour and esteem, we thank and praise You.

May Your name be praised for ever by every living being.

Praised are You YHWH, for the Shabbat and its set apartness.

HA-TEHILLIM

The Tehillim is the weekly portion of the Psalms that is read on the Shabbat. The word Tehillim literally means "Praise." This is what is said before reading the Tehillim and after reading the Tehillim on the Shabbat. It can also be said at any time you read Tehillim.

HA-TEHILLIM

The blessing before the reading of the Tehillim

Barukh Atah יהוה, Eloheinu Melech haOlam, Asher kid'shanu b'mitzvotav v'tzivanu likro et hahalel.

Praised are You YHWH, our Elohim King of the Universe, Who has sanctified us us with His commandments and commanded us to Praise Him with the Psalms.

The blessing after the reading of the Tehillim

Y'hiyu l'ratzon im'rei fi v'hegyon libi l'fanekha, יהוה tzuri v'goali. Amein.

May the words of my mouth and the meditations of my heart be acceptable to You YHWH, my rock and my redeemer. Amein. (Tehillim (Psalm) 19:15).

KETUVIM NETZARIM

The Ketuvim Netzarim literally means "the writings of the Nazarenes" who were the authors of the Brit Chadashah or the Renewed Covenant. The Ketuvim Netzarim is the weekly portion of the Renewed Covenant that is read on the Shabbat. This is what is said before reading the Brit Chadashah and after reading the Brit Chadashah on the Shabbat. It can also be said at any time you read the Brit Chadashah.

KETUVIM NETZARIM

The blessing before the reading of the Brit Chadashah

Barukh Atah יהוה, Eloheinu Melech haOlam, Asher diber-lanu k'Yeshua Hamasheeach asher d'var hacha-yim.

Praised are You YHWH, our Elohim King of the Universe, Who has spoken to us as Yeshua the Messiah, Who is the word of life.

The blessing after the reading of the Brit Chadashah

Barukh Atah יהוה, Eloheinu Melech haOlam, Asher asah et d'varo or lagoyim v'yaysha l'Yisra'el.

Praised are You YHWH, our Elohim King of the Universe, Who has made His word a light to the nations and salvation to Yisra'el.

BIRKAT HA-MAZON

The commandment to thank YHWH after a meal is of Scriptural origin: *"And you shall eat and you shall be satisfied and you shall bless יהוה, your Elohim for the goodly land that יהוה gave you"* Devarim (Deuteronomy) 8:10. Birkat Ha'mazon means grace after meals. We have provided the short and long form of the prayer.

BIRKAT HA-MAZON

The prayer of thanksgiving (shortform)

B'reekh Rach'man Maray D'ha'ee Peeta (Aramaic).

We thank You, O Merciful One, Provider of this food.

Barukh Harachman Mazon ha'acilah Hazot (Hebrew).

Praised be the Merciful One, Provider of this food.

Harachaman, Hu yishlach b'rakha m'ruba babayit hazeh v'al shulkhan zeh she'achalnu alav. Amein.

May the Merciful One send abundant blessing upon this dwelling and the table at which we have eaten. Amein.

The prayer of thanksgiving (Longform)

Barukh Atah יהוה, Eloheinu Melech haOlam, hazan et ha'olam kulo b'tuvo b'chayn b'chesaid uv'ra'chameem, hu notayn lechem l'khol-basar, ki l'olam chasdo, uv'tuvo hagadol tameed lo chasar lanu v'al yech'sar lanu mazon l'olam va'ed. Ba'avur sh'mo hagadol, ki hu El zan um'far'nays lakol, umayteev lakol u'maykheen mazon l'chol-b'reeyotav asher bara.
Barukh Atah יהוה, hazan et hakol. Amein.

Praised are You YHWH, our Elohim King of the Universe, Who sustains the entire world with goodness, kindness and mercy. Giving bread to all creatures and Whoes mercies is everlasting. Through Your abundant goodness we have not lacked sustenance and may we not lack Your provision forever, for the sake of Your Great Name. Elohim sustains all, does good to all, and provides bread for all creatures that are created.
Praised is YHWH, Who provides food for all. Amein.

V'al hakol יהוה *Eloheinu ananchu modem lakh um-var'khim otakh yitbarakh shimcha b'fi khol chai tamid l'olam va'ed, kakatuv: V'akhalta v'savata uvayrakhta et* יהוה *Elohekha al ha-aretz hatova asher natan lakh. Barukh Atah* יהוה, *al ha-aretz v'al hamazon. Amein.*

For all these blessings we thank you YHWH our Elohim with praise. May Elohim's name be praised by every living being forever, as it is written: *"And you shall eat and you shall be satisfied and you shall bless* יהוה, *your Elohim for the goodly land that* יהוה *gave you."* Amein.

BIRKHOT

Birkhot is the plural form of bless. Birkhot (blessings) generally falls into one of three categories:

1. *Birkhot hanehenin* - those said before enjoying a material pleasure, such as eating and drinking.
2. *Birkhot ha-mitzvot* - those recited before performing a mitzvah (a commandment) such as lighting a candle.
3. *Birkhot hada'ah* - those said at special times and events such as seeing a rainbow or hearing thunder.

In Hebrew we always praise or bless the originator and creator of life YHWH and not the subject or object of His creation. Rabbinical teaching exhort Torah keepers to make at least 100 blessings daily, much of which is in prayer liturgy.

The blessing when eating bread

Barukh Atah יהוה, Eloheinu melech haOlam, ha'motzi lechem min ha'aretz.

Praised are You YHWH, our Elohim King of the Universe, You bring forth the bread from the earth.

The blessing when drinking grape juice

Barukh Atah יהוה, Elohenu Melech haOlam, Boray pri hagafen.

Praised are You YHWH, our Elohim King of the Universe, Creator of the fruit of the vine.

The blessing when washing your hands

Barukh Atah יהוה, Eloheinu Melech haOlam, Asher kid'shanu b'mitz'votav, v'tzivanu al n'tilat yadayim.

Praised are You YHWH, our Elohim King of the Universe, Who has sanctified us us with the commandments and commanded us to wash our hands.

The blessing when smelling fragrant spices

Barukh Atah יהוה, Eloheinu Melech haOlam, Boray minay vesamim.

Praised are You YHWH, our Elohim King of the Universe, Creator of the different spices.

The blessing when lighting a fire

Barukh Atah יהוה, Eloheinu Melech haOlam, Boray Me'oray ha'aysh.

Praised are You YHWH, our Elohim King of the Universe, Creator of the fire's lights.

The blessing when eating fruit of a tree

Barukh Atah יהוה, Eloheinu Melech haOlam, Boray pri ha'eytz.

Praised are You YHWH, our Elohim King of the Universe, Who creates the fruits of the tree.

The blessing when eating products created from various types of wheat and grains

Barukh Atah יהוה, Eloheinu Melech haOlam, Boray meenay m'zonot.

Praised are You YHWH, our Elohim King of the Universe, Who creates various forms of nourishments.

The blessing when drinking any other drink except grape juice or eating any other food except wheat and grains

Barukh Atah יהוה, Eloheinu Melech haOlam, Shehakol nihya bid'varo.

Praised are You YHWH, our Elohim King of the Universe, Whose word caused everything to be.

The blessing when eating vegetables

Barukh Atah יהוה, Eloheinu Melech haOlam, Boray pri ha'adama.

Praised are You YHWH, our Elohim King of the Universe, Who creates the fruit of the ground.

The blessing when smelling fragrant herbs

Barukh Atah יהוה, Eloheinu Melech haOlam, Boray minay is vay v'samin.

Praised are You YHWH, our Elohim King of the Universe, Who Creates fragrant herbs.

The blessing when smelling fragrant plants or flowers

Barukh Atah יהוה, Eloheinu Melech haOlam, Boray atzay v'samin.

Praised are You YHWH, our Elohim King of the Universe, Who Creates fragrant plants.

The blessing when smelling a pleasant fruit

Barukh Atah יהוה, Eloheinu Melech haOlam, Hanotayn rayach tov bapayrot.

Praised are You YHWH, our Elohim King of the Universe, Who gives pleasant aroma to fruits.

The blessing when seeing wonderful displays of nature like lighting, or seeing majestic mountains and rivers etc.

Barukh Atah יהוה, Eloheinu Melech haOlam, Osay ma'asay v'raysheet.

Praised are You YHWH, our Elohim King of the Universe, Who creates wonderful displays of creation.

The blessing when hearing the sound of thunder

Barukh Atah יהוה, Eloheinu Melech haOlam, Shekocho ug'vurato malay olam.

Praised are You YHWH, our Elohim King of the Universe, Whose power and might fill the World.

The blessing when seeing wonderful creations in the Universe like planets, comets, shooting stars etc.

Barukh Atah יהוה, Eloheinu Melech haOlam, Shekocho ug'vurato malay olam.

Praised are You יהוה, our Elohim King of the Universe, for His power and might fill the Universe.

The blessing when seeing a rainbow

Barukh Atah יהוה, Eloheinu Melech haOlam, Zokhayr hab'reet v'ne'eman biv'reeto v'kaiyom b'ma'amaro.

Praised are You YHWH, our Elohim King of the Universe, Who remembers His Covenant and is faithful to His covenant and fulfils His Word.

The blessing when seeing the Ocean or a great span of water

Barukh Atah יהוה, Eloheinu Melech haOlam, She'asa et-hayam hagadol.

Praised are You YHWH, our Elohim King of the Universe, Who creates the great oceans.

The blessing when seeing a beautiful tree or animals

Barukh Atah יהוה, *Eloheinu Melech haOlam, Shekakha lo b'olamo.*

Praised are You YHWH, our Elohim King of the Universe, Who has such as these in the World.

The blessing when seeing trees begin to blossom

Barukh Atah יהוה, *Eloheinu Melech haOlam, Shelo chisar b'olamo davar, uvara vo b'reeot tovot v'ilanot tovim l'hanot bahem b'nay adam.*

Praised are You YHWH, our Elohim King of the Universe, Who has made the World complete and has produced such beautiful creations and trees so that we might derive pleasure from them.

The blessing when hearing or seeing good tidings

Barukh Atah יהוה, *Eloheinu Melech haOlam, ha'tov v'hamayteev.*

Praised are You YHWH, our Elohim King of the Universe, Who is good and does good.

The blessing when hearing or seeing tragic events

Barukh Atah יהוה, *Eloheinu Melech haOlam, Dayan ha'emet.*

Praised are You YHWH, our Elohim King of the Universe, Who is Judge of truth.

The blessing when having narrowly escaped danger, recovering from serious illness or after coming through safely after a long journey

Barukh Atah יהוה, Eloheinu Melech haOlam, haGomel l'chayavim tovim sheg'malanee kol tov.

Praised are You YHWH, our Elohim King of the Universe, Who has grants favours to the undeserving, Who has granted me all kindness.

The blessing when erecting a structure or railing

Barukh Atah יהוה, Eloheinu Melech haOlam, Asher kid'shanu b'mitz'votav, v'tzivanu la'asot ma'ke.

Praised are You YHWH, our Elohim King of the Universe, Who has sanctified us us with the commandments and commanded us to erect a structure.

The blessing during a woman's monthly immersion

Barukh Atah יהוה, Eloheinu Melech haOlam, Asher kid'shanu b'mitz'votav, v'tzivanu al hat'veela.

Praised are You YHWH, our Elohim King of the Universe, Who has sanctified us with the commandments and commanded us concerning immersion.

The blessing when washing a cooking utensil (utensils)

Barukh Atah יהוה, Eloheinu Melech haOlam, Asher kid'shanu b'mitz'votav, al t'veelat kaylee (kaylim).

Praised are You YHWH, our Elohim King of the Universe, Who has sanctified us with the commandments and commanded us concerning the immersion of a cooking utensil (utensils).

The blessing when you obtain something new

Barukh Atah יהוה, Eloheinu Melech haOlam, Sheshecheyanu v'keey'manu v'hurgee'anu laz'man hazeh.

Praised are You YHWH, our Elohim King of the Universe, Who has kept us in life, has sustained us, and brought us to this joyous time.

The blessing when you put on new clothes

Barukh Atah יהוה, Eloheinu Melech haOlam, Malbeesh arumim.

Praised are You, YHWH our Elohim King of the Universe, Who clothes those who have a need.

The blessing when you met a great Torah scholar or teacher

Barukh Atah יהוה, Eloheinu Melech haOlam, Shechalak maychokhmat leeray-av.

Praised are You YHWH, our Elohim King of the Universe, Who have given of His wisdom to those who receive Him.

The blessing when you met a person of great secular wisdom

Barukh Atah יהוה, Eloheinu Melech haOlam, Shenatan matchokhmato l'vasar vadam.

Praised are You YHWH, our Elohim King of the Universe, Who has imparted His wisdom to flesh and blood.

The blessing before studying the Torah

Barukh Atah יהוה, Eloheinu Melech haOlam, Asher k'dishanu b'mitzvotav v'tzivanu la'asok b'divrei Torah.

Praised are You YHWH, our Elohim Ruler of the Universe, Who sanctified us with mitzvot and commands us to engage in the study of Torah.

The blessing before reciting a Psalm or a Hymn of praise and thanksgiving

Barukh Atah יהוה, Eloheinu Melech haOlam, Asher kidshanu b'mitzvotav v'tzivanu likro et hahalel.

Praised are You YHWH, our Elohim King of the Universe, Who has sanctified us with His commandments and commanded us to praise Him with Psalms.

MEZUZAH

The mitzvah (command) to place a mezuzah upon the door posts of the house is derived from Devarim (Deuteronomy) 6:4-9. The words of the Shema are written on a tiny scroll of parchment, along with the words of a companion passage Devarim (Deuteronomy) 11:13-21. On the back of the Scroll the name of YHWH is written in Hebrew. This scroll is the placed in a case and affixed to the right side of the door on a 45 degree angle slanting to the right. Every time you pass through the door with a mezuzah on it, you touch the mezuzah and then kiss your finders reminding you of this mitzvah and to bless this house.

MEZUZAH

The blessing for the mezuzah scroll

Just before attaching the mezuzah say:

Barukh Atah יהוה, *Eloheinu Melech haOlam, Asher kidshanu b'mitzvotav v'tzivanu lik'boa m'zuzah.*

Praised are You YHWH, our Elohim King of the Universe, Who sanctified us with Mitzvot, and commands us to affix mezuzah.

ABOUT NO MANS ZONE

NO MANS ZONE was founded on the 70th Jubilee year 2009, the Jewish year 5769.

The Purpose of NMZ is set forth in these Scriptures:

NMZ Vision: Yeshayahu (Isaiah) 40:1-9, Yechezkel (Ezekiel) 37.

NMZ Mission: Yeshayahu (Isaiah) 61, Yirmeyahu (Jeremiah) 31.

NMZ Goal: Mattityahu (Matthew) 10:5-10, Marqus (Mark) 16:15-18.

NOTES

NOTES

For further information and
for other publications contact

WWW.NOMANSZONE.ORG

Made in the USA
San Bernardino, CA
03 January 2015